ANXIETY AND

MW01487909

IN RELATIONSHIP

The Definitive Self-Help Guide to Boost Your Self-Esteem and Eliminate Couples Conflicts, Insecurity, Jealousy, Insecure Attachment, and Negative Thinking

Felicity Moore

By reading this document, the reader agrees that under no circumstances is the author responsible for any losses, direct or indirect, which are incurred as a result of the use of information contained within this document, including, but not limited to, — errors, omissions, or inaccuracies.

Table of contents

Book 1

ANXIETY IN RELATIONSHIP

How to Overcome Anxiety, Negative Thinking, Jealousy, Manage Insecurity and Attachment. Discover How to Eliminate Couples Conflicts to Establish Better Relationships

INTRODUCTION

Being in a relationship with someone because you have trouble with anxiety or an anxiety disorder can be very depressing in itself. Sometimes, you can get the feeling that fear in the relationship is a third party, an invisible personality that falls between you and your partner. This person is accountable for all the uncertainty and difficulties in your relationship that you face.

Periods of distress, sensations of dread or a sensation of being stressed, uneasy, or tense may be triggered by anxiety. Anxiety will take over your mind and extend into many other aspects of your life, influencing your thinking and success in this manner. It infuses connections with a strain and places them at considerable risk. The confidence and bond that any relationship wants is disrupted when anxiety thrives in a relationship. It takes your mind off the most important facets of your relationship as fear sets in, and you become less attuned to your partner's wishes and preferences. Fear and fear have become the order of the day.

"More dreams than failure ever will kill insecurity." Suzy Kassem. Anxiety is a psychiatric disorder you are all too well aware of. As soon as the absence of focus, hyperventilation, irritability, sweating, elevated heart rate, worry, fear of imminent disaster, nausea, shaking, and racing thoughts starts, you know the symptoms. You fear the moment your anxiety spikes because you fail to control it, particularly when you are in public. You believe like you are the only one struggling with fear, but in the United States, it is the most prevalent type of psychiatric disorder. About 40 million persons 18 years and older per year are afflicted by these conditions. Unfortunately, fewer than 40 percent seek the assistance they need to feel ashamed for different reasons, such as lack of health care.

You may find that at some periods of your life, your anxiety creeps up. When you are going to introduce your friends, for instance, when your professor asks you to answer a question, or when you are having difficulty with your significant other. In a regular basis, you may even experience discomfort, no matter what you are doing or with whom you are. Since in many aspects of their life, fear influences millions of people.

Some of the distress people had was due to previous baggage or personal insecurities in their relationship. You are feeling insecurities in your relationship much like anyone else, increasing your stress and worries. Environmental tension, biology, confrontation, worried about failing your spouse or someone else, mistrust, dependence, and childhood abuse are some of the most important sources of vulnerability.

Fear of abandonment is one of the main reasons people add fear into their relationships. This anxiety can emerge from feeling rejected as a child by a parent or for a multitude of other causes. Feeling breakup anxiety, feeling incapable of love, feeling vulnerable, vulnerability to critique, going quickly on so you do not get addicted to one person, and striving to satisfy are some of the strongest signs of this feeling.

Another common factor that this book would focus a lot of time on is envy. While being a little jealous is common, extreme jealousy can be harmful to a relationship's wellbeing. Studies reveal, for instance, that about 90% of men and 60% of women fantasize about someone they have met. Both 70% of men and women claim, however, that they have often lied to their partner so that they might or would not get jealous. Yet envy would easily become an issue and lead to an abusive relationship, proven by 70% of men and women that when it came to a jealous condition in their relationship, they confessed to lying.

Understanding that focusing on problems such as jealousy and fear of abandonment is not straightforward, but trying to repair yourself and your relationship is crucial. Your friendship is happy because you are happy. For both you and your partner, this helps in a happier and safe life and friendship. However, it will also help not only help your romantic relationship to solve your challenges; it will help relationships with your siblings, parents, friends, colleagues, and everyone else you constantly communicate with.

You feel stressed, concerned about what is going on but you find it hard to really pay attention to what is going on. Your companion may feel as if you are not there when this happens. You may find it hard to express your true feelings when you are insecure in your relationship. Anxiety gets more severe if you do not convey what you really want or need, and your feelings can threaten to run out of control if you try to bottle them up. This adds to you feeling defensive and overwhelmed.

Intimate encounters are capable of representing the best and worst of us all. They are mirrors, which can fuel or relax our struggles. Anxiety is a toxin that can rob the pleasure of two people who belong together and the bond between them. You may have been with your partner for a long period, but you are constantly dealing with the fact that your partner does not live up to your standards and will not be able to fill your heart with the void. Perhaps you suspect, too, that you are part of the problem.

Maybe you are uncomfortable in love; you feel desperately alone and want to be joined by a friend and lover through the thrill and journey of life.

You are always questioning if someone is still there for you, if you let your guard down and you are yourself. Through your weakness, will you be able to find warmth, reassurance, and support from them? At any opportunity, you contemplate these things.

The primary purpose is to conquer any anxiety you have experienced or are actually feeling in your relationships. Many individuals have been able to confront their fears, look them in the eye, and overcome any anxiety and restriction that prevents their joy. You would have overcome a big part of the fear that has been destroying your relationships as you deliberately follow all that has been written here and take all the exercises to heart.

In lust, you will start to feel less insecure and attached.

To remove such patterns, you will be able to recognise irrational behaviors that cause fear and take meaningful and constructive action.

Know that you can enjoy a safe, wholesome, and valuable sex life, a relationship in which you are not vulnerable and do not feel uncomfortable or tied. You will have a loving relationship in which, with your partner doing the same, you see yourself increasing and adding positive value.

CHAPTER 1

Anxiety and Insecurity in Relationships

Anxiety is both a serious problem and a mental health condition, which if not correctly tested, will lead to a number of other issues. From time to time, though, everyone experiences anxiety, and it only becomes a problem if it is serious.

Anxiety will affect your relationships adversely, particularly if you spend a great deal of time stressing and worried about anything that could go wrong or has already gone wrong with the relationship. When you are too nervous in a relationship, here are some questions that might go through your mind:

- What if as much as I love them, they don't love me?
- What if they don't love me as much as I love them?
- What if they're lying to me?
- What if they're cheating on me?
- What if I'm not good enough in the future for them?
- What if they find someone else more attractive?
- What if their family doesn't love me?
- What if they die?
- What if my anxiety ruins our relationship? (Anxiety about anxiety)

- What if we break up?
- What if they bail out on me?

It is common to have any of these thoughts, particularly in a new relationship.

However, it may be a symptom of anxiety disorders or an anxiety disorder when feelings like these come to your mind often. The degree at which you continually ruminate on the above-mentioned questions and other related questions decide how deep you have gone through an anxiety problem. In your relationship, it will also decide how vulnerable you are. In different bodily forms, these nervous feelings are expressed and present as signs such as shortness of breath, insomnia, and anxiety or heart attacks.

You may find that you cause a panic attack if you think this way, in which your heart may begin to pound quickly, a hard lump forms in your chest, and you start trembling all over your body. Those are the biochemical symptoms of an anxiety disorder that you suffer from. These nervous feelings cause your companion to act in ways that further stress you out and strain the relationship in certain instances.

This is because to your partner you are open enough that they can see you are vulnerable. This gives them a deceptive edge on you to manipulate and turn situations in ways that do not normally mean a thing, but would inevitably damage you and reinforce one or two of your nervous convictions. You are nervous and stressed about being the first to start a conversation all the time, for instance.

In your head, you feel sick because your partner does not like you and they do not take the first step of talking as much as you do. The fear builds up and gains traction, and if you do not reach out first, you tend to think they might never talk with you or call you up. You realize it is a smart idea to go silent on them for a bit in order to address this fear.

This forces your partner to engage with you, reaching out a couple times before you feel secure knowing that they are going to make the effort. This proof encourages you to doubt the nervous, unfounded conviction that they are not going to reach out first. This is not a healthy technique, however. The easiest way to overcome anxiety disorder is to deal with the root cause of anxiety, restore your confidence, and leave you with a free and joyful life. Emotionally intense relationships are personal.

This is due to the closeness with another person that you share. Alas, the closeness often leaves you helpless and can contribute to anxiety and insecurity. Anxiety is fear of the unknown, while self-doubt and the lack of self-confidence are uncertainty. Many occasions, if not adequately handled, uncertainty graduates into fear. It is also important to remember that you grow low self-esteem and eventually insecurity sets in as you stress excessively in your relationship.

You start to see in a negative light the motives or actions of your partner; you see your partner as intimidating or critical. Other signs of extreme anxiety disorder can include:

- A feeling of restlessness
- Tensed muscles
- Difficulty concentrating or remembering
- Procrastinating or having trouble making decisions
- Worry that leads to repeatedly asking for reassurance
- Inability to get enough sleep and rest

They can also create nervous thoughts and emotions, because relationships are very beautiful and pleasurable.

At any point of the relationship, these thoughts will emerge. The thought of finding the right person and being in a relationship will already create fear for you, which you have to contend with, if you are not in a relationship yet. Insecurity is an inner sense of somehow not being adequate or feeling threatened.

For one time or another, we have all felt it. Getting feelings of self-doubt occasionally is very common, but constant depression will sabotage your life's success and wreck your romantic relationships. Extreme fear steals the equilibrium and stops you from being able to communicate in a relaxed and authentic manner with your mate.

Jealousy, false allegations, snooping, loss of faith, and finding reassurance and affirmation can be the resulting behavior that emerge from fear. Such traits are not conducive to a stable friendship and will drive your wife further. Many individuals conclude the insecurity derives from their spouses' behavior or inaction.

The irony is much fear comes from inside you. When you equate yourself to other persons negatively and judge yourself critically in your inner critical voice, you develop insecurity. In your relationship, many of the insecurities are focused on unfounded feelings and concerns that you are not good enough and that you are not able to make anyone else happy. However, that is not real! One thing you should do is to start taking stock of your worth as you start to experience the uncomfortable feeling of being nervous.

Insecurity lets you rely on something inside you that you believe is missing. Each partner brings various strengths and qualities that complement each other in the healthiest relationships. Take stock of the importance you give to your partner in order to overcome your vulnerability. Personality and great character are important attributes for a relationship's overall wellbeing. To overcome any insecurity you face in your relationship, building your self-esteem is also crucial.

In order not to continually gain approval from anyone else, it is important that you feel confident about who you are on the inside. Inside yourself, you are complete and by your deeds and acts, you must let your dignity and self-worth shine brightly. You give them the key to your joy and you motivate them while your well-being depends on someone else. This could be very unhealthy for your wife to tolerate and definitely does not work well for a relationship. One way to develop your self-confidence is to silence your inner detractors and reflect on good qualities of your mind and focus. Look in the mirror and utter encouraging things about yourself - staring in the eye as you do this has a stronger effect than merely reminding yourself that you are deserving of love in your head.

You should also be able to retain your sense of self-identity and tend to your emotional well-being. If you were doing a fine job of providing about your physical, social and emotional needs before the relationship, this should not end now simply because you are in a relationship. You should preserve your individuality and not allow yourself to turn into someone who is needy or attached. You therefore become a more engaging and desirable companion by becoming an autonomous person who has a life and personality outside of the relationship. When you are in a relationship, your life must continue to go forward and make significant progress. It is not the final stage of your life to be in a relationship, and you can strive to be motivated to accomplish further milestones, which will help endear you to your partner.

Cultivating and cultivating great friendships, finding time for your own friends, passions, and activities, retaining financial freedom, continually enhancing yourself, and setting high expectations for your goals are several ways of preserving your independence.

- UNDERSTANDING WHY YOU FEEL ANXIOUS, INSECURE AND ATTACHED IN RELATIONSHIPS

When you start a relationship, you will panic and stress up with multiple questions in your mind at the initial point, begging for answers. You are starting to think:

- "Does he/she really like me?"
- "Will this work out?"
- "How serious will this get?"

It is sad to note that when you are riddled by fear, these issues do not diminish in the later stages of the relationship. The more and more personal you get in a relationship, the greater the strength of the anxiety seen in such a relationship can be as a matter of fact.

Worry, tension and anxiety will leave you feeling lonely and unhappy about your relationships. You can build a divide between yourself and your loved one unknowingly. Another extreme effect of fear is the potential to absolutely make one give up on passion. That is devastating, because love is a very lovely thing. In a relationship, it is important to really understand what makes you so nervous and why you feel so vulnerable and attached.

In many ways, being in love places a demand on you in more ways than you can think. The more a human you cherish, the more you stand to lose. How fucking ironic is that? This deep feeling of love and the heavy feelings that knowingly and implicitly come with it build the fear of being hurt and the fear of the unknown inside you.

Oddly enough, this dread comes as a result of being treated in your relationship precisely how you expect to be treated. Anxiety may set in when you begin to experience love as it should be, or when you are handled in a tender and loving way that is foreign to you.

It is not just the incidents that arise between you and your partner that contribute to anxiety, more frequently than not. It is the thoughts you think to yourself about those incidents that inevitably contribute to distress and fill your mind. Your strongest critic, who is also the "mean coach" in your mind, will be willing to judge you and give you negative advice that will eventually fuel your fear of intimacy. It is this average reviewer who tells you that:

- "You are not smart; he/she would soon get bored of you."
- "You will never meet anyone who will love you, so why try?"
- "Don't trust him; he's probably searching for a better person."
- "She doesn't really love you. Get out before you get hurt."

The cruel coach in your mind is controlling you and turning you against yourself and the ones you love. Hostility is promoted, and you quickly learn that you are paranoid. Every step your partner takes, you begin to doubt, which decreases your self-esteem and drives unhealthy levels of mistrust, defensiveness, envy, anxiety, and tension.

What this coach means in your brain is continuously supplying you with ideas that jeopardize your happiness and making you think about your friendship instead of simply letting you enjoy it. You get terribly disconnected from the actual relationship, which requires good contact and affection with your partner, as you start to concentrate too hard on these unhealthy feelings.

You quickly find that you are listening to needless difficulties and uttering disgusting and harmful remarks. You can have become childish or parental with your partner.

Your companion, for instance, arrives home from work and does not have a strong appetite, so they turn down dinner respectfully. "After some time sitting alone, your inner critic goes on a rampage and asks, "Why can he deny my food? What did he eat the whole day? Who brought food for him at work? Should I trust him for real? These thoughts will grow constantly in your head until you are insecure, angry, and temperamental by the next morning. You can start acting cold or furious, and your partner may be turned off by this, leaving them irritated and defensive. They are not going to know what is going on in your brain, so it is going to look like your action is coming out of nowhere.

You have effectively changed the dynamics of your friendship in just a couple of hours. You may waste an entire day feeling distracted and pulled away from each other instead of savoring the time you spend together. What you have just done is initiate the gap you dreaded so much and throne it. The circumstance itself is not the blame factor for this turn of events - it is the vital inner voice that clouded your emotions, skewed your views, suggested bad opinions to you and directed you to a catastrophic direction as a consequence.

What you do not know and what your inner critic doesn't tell you is that you are tougher and more robust than you believe when it comes to the problems that you care over so much in your partnership. The truth is that the hurts, rejections, and disappointments you are so afraid of can be handled. We are made in such a manner that it is possible to absorb, recover from and cope with negative conditions. You are able to feel suffering, in the end, recover, and come out better. Nevertheless the mean coach in your mind, the inner cynical voice, keeps you under pressure more frequently than not and makes reality seem like a disaster. It generates non-existent situations in your imagination and pulls forth risks that are not tangible. In addition, if there are genuine challenges and unstable circumstances in life, the inner voice in your head will magnify these situations and rip you apart in ways that you do not deserve. The truth of the situation will be totally misrepresented and will dampen your own resilience and resolve. It will still supply you with unpleasant opinions and advice.

However, because of your own personal experiences and what you have adapted to over time, the vital voices you hear in your head are created. There is a propensity in our acts to get too attached and desperate when you feel stressed or nervous. Possessiveness and authority over your mate set in. You may sense an interference into your relationship, on the other hand. You can begin to withdraw and disconnect from your emotional needs from your partner. You can tend to behave unwanted or removed.

Your early attachment styles may derive from these patterns of responding to problems. These trends of style affect how you respond to your needs and how you get them met.

Any vital inner voices are talking about you, your partner, and your experiences. These inner voices are created by early attitudes in your family, among your peers, or in society that you were introduced to. The inner criticism of all is distinct; there are some typical inner critical voices, however.

Inner Voices that are Critical about the Relationship:

- ✓ Most people end up getting hurt.
- ✓ Relationships never work out.

Inner Voices that are Critical about Your Partner:

- ✓ He is probably cheating on you.
- ✓ You cannot trust her.
- ✓ Men are so insensitive, unreliable, and selfish.

Inner Voices about Yourself:

- ✓ You are better off on your own.
- ✓ It is your fault if he gets upset.
- ✓ You always screw things up.
- ✓ You have to keep him interested.
- ✓ He does not really care about you.

If you listen to your inner self, the resulting consequence is a relationship filled with fear, which will in several ways mar your sex life. You may avoid feeling like the confident and independent person you were when you first began the relationship if you give in to this fear. This will make you thin out, break apart, causing jealousy, and fear more. Attachment and neediness are created, which place a strain on the relationship.

In your relationship, this anxiety condition will continue to leave you feeling threatened and you may therefore begin to overpower or manipulate your partner. Perhaps to minimize your own insecurities, you find yourself setting rules for what they can or can not do. This may lead to a sense of your partner's withdrawal and resentment.

You can tend to shield yourself by being cold and distant to protect yourself when you allow yourself to feel insecure in a relationship, and this may be painful for your partner. This gap will also stir up your partner's insecurity.

Your reaction to fear is often more akin to violence. Without even noticing it you can yell and scream at your partner. You have to pay conscious attention to how often of your acts are a direct reaction to your mate, and how much your inner analytical voice reacts to them.

• SIGNS OF INSECURE ATTACHMENT

As a product of vulnerability, there are a few behaviors that are brought on by attachments. Because of unreliable relations, a number of undesirable practices will turn up in early adolescence.

1. Too Demanding

You do not want your buddy, for instance, to get things done without you. Your desire is to blow away much of your time together and their spare time. To the detriment of other friendships and partnerships, you request their time and thought.

2. Doubt or Jealousy

You are wary of the actions of your partner or companion, for example, and the general public they interact with. In the professional world, you doubt their work relationships and who they associate with. As you dread that they may abandon you for another human, you are wary of everyone who you believe they are getting too close to.

3. Absence of Emotional Intimacy

Your companion or girlfriend, for example, thinks, as they can't really draw close to you. They depict you as someone who "sets up dividers" or claims that you are typically tough to draw inwardly close to.

4. Enthusiastic Dependency

For your enthusiastic success, you count on your companion or spouse. Your goal is to ensure that your pleasure comes from your friendship. In the case that you are angry, this is because you think your partner or friend is not happy with you.

5. Frightful

In your intimate relationships, you want closeness. Your understanding, though, has been that they would harm you in the event that you come too close to your loved one. This makes you have a combination of emotions. Your avoidance of being excessively close, because you would like not to be harmed, allows your relationship to suffer. You pull your partner close and then force them away as it becomes too much."

6. Absence of Trust

Out of fear that they might undermine you or abandon you, you do not confide in your friend. You are scared you could say something to them or show a part of yourself that they are not going to accept and encourage them to end the relationship.

7. Anger Issues

In a friendship, becoming overly upset is often a symptom of unstable connection. It indicates that you are not willing to accept your partner or you are fed up with their excesses when you want a confrontation over a dispute that could be settled amicably. This behaviour, if not resolved, will adversely affect the relationship.

Let me conclude by saying that you continue to drive your partner away from you as you behave out your insecurities, thereby forming a prophecy that is self-fulfilling. By self-fulfilling prophecy, I mean validating those destructive thoughts that come to your mind, also known as your inner voice, and give life to them. It's beginning to seem like the voice was right after all. However, no, it hasn't been right. The fight is internal and goes on irrespective of the conditions. Your life might really be like a fairy tale when you deal with fear, but that inner voice would always have something negative to find out. Dealing with your insecurities is vital without pulling your partner into them. After taking two steps, you will do this: expose the origins of your insecurities and explore what ultimately contributed to them. Challenge the inner negative voice and the mean coach who obstructs the relationship's free flow of affection.

• DIFFERENT TYPES OF ANXIETY

According to a set of factors varying from age, genetic material, life conditions, etc., anxiety expresses itself differently in each person.

There may be various forms of fear, separated or mixed from each other. In addition, you may get panic problems and phobias and obsessive-compulsive disorder or hypochondria. The main thing is that you find the proper diagnosis and learn where to start if you have either of these forms of anxiety.

Keep in mind that we all have a little bit of all of this, so if anything is already distracting you from loving life and doing your usual things, you're about to get help. The anxiety types are:

1. Social Anxiety Disorder

Best known as social phobia, it is characterized by extreme and constant fear of one or more social circumstances in which the person is, or has to interact with strangers, subjected to the potential appraisal of others.

The biggest fear of these people is that they act in front of others in an embarrassing or shameful manner, or that they know they are nervous. It means avoiding or living social environments of almost all sorts, followed by visible signs of anxiety that they tend to conceal.

In the end, it allows the person with this disorder to have challenges in their everyday life: no social entity, job or school difficulty, or distress due to their phobia.

It takes six months or longer for a diagnosis to be made. It is one of the most prominent causes of anxiety, being found in around 2-3% of the general population.

2. Chronic Concern

Your family, your fitness, your job, your economy all matter to you. You get the feeling that something bad, even though you don't know what the problem is is going to happen to you. At the sight of these matters, your stomach is constantly churning.

The dilemma is mainly about elements of the future, but it may be about the past as well. Imagine the worse situations, and it helps you live as if what you are thinking about is happening now.

For instance: That your kids don't come home on schedule, because you're concerned about what could happen to them Jealousy or you're worried about what your partner is doing or who he's worrying about not getting money in the future or because it doesn't hit you.

3. Fears and Phobias

Fear is born of the fact that you feel at risk, and these feelings generally exist only in your head. It could be something that's happened to you or something you've seen that's happened to someone. In which you magnify risk, anxiety is based on unrealistic expectations and assumptions.

Terror is born in fear, and fear is an instinct that threatens your life, however, at the moment we have worries that are not a threat, but that keep it from happening at all costs.

Phobias are an extreme anxiety created by painful events or by simply ignoring what began with fear for a long time. Blood, heights, elevators, walking, air transport, snakes, spiders, floods, bridges, or being locked up indoors may be needle phobia. If you try to believe that this might happen, the hate would not encourage you to get close or so, so you start to experience odd and uncomfortable sensations in your body instantly.

Fear of isolation, gloom, insecurity, syringe phobia, blood, snakes, closed spaces, for example.

4. Anxiety about Acting

Whenever you have to take a test, act or do something in front of other persons or participate in a sporting event, you freeze.

Anxiety to talk in public: anytime you have to speak in front of a group of people, you get anxious and you think to yourself, "everyone is going to realize that I'm nervous, my mind will go blank, and I'll make a fool of myself, I'm going to fall ill" etc.

5. Shyness

In social events, you feel awkward and rushed when you say to yourself, "everyone seems charming and relaxed, but I have nothing interesting to say." "Most likely, they realize how shy I am and how out of place I feel" "They must think I'm a kind of weird or failed type" "I'm the only one who feels like this, what's happening to me?"

You have a difficult time confronting other persons, especially those of the opposite sex. You have a barrier that keeps you from asking someone what you think and sharing your emotions that you don't have a lot of trust. It is easier to go unnoticed than to draw scrutiny, you say, but deep down, you want someone to give you some attention.

6. Panic Attack

You are feeling extreme, frightening panic attacks that sound like they are only emerging and instantly attacking you, like lightning. You feel dizzy during raids, your pulse is racing, your fingertips are tingling. "Or am I dying?" "I can't breathe! What if I drown?"

You're struggling to hang on to survival, and you may be running to the closest emergency room in the hospital. In a short time, the sensation of fear fades as mysteriously as it arrived, but you are absent with a curious feeling, confused, frightened and sometimes embarrassed. Are you thinking what happens and when it is going to happen again, and what is going to happen to me?

Doctors tell you that you are in great shape, that you ought to learn how to relax, and that they might give you a tablet of Rivotril. However, there is always the terror. There is no getting anywhere from the restlessness and sense of strangeness.

7. Selective Mutism

Selective mutism is a recent addition to DSM-V and is the inability, when it should be, complete, to start a discussion or respond to others. In other words, people influenced by selective mutism are not able to communicate like those in particular social spheres, nor in others.

When they are at home with their nearest friends, for example, they have no trouble holding conversations, but they can not do so in other environments (school, for example). In short, except for those well-known people for whom you have a lot of confidence, it might be assumed that some people have a phobia that someone could hear you speaking about.

Other means of talking are also developing nodding, gestures, whispering in the ear, and through drawing. They are preserved several times over time by reinforcing those who interpret their expressions or speak with them; allowing those affected not to heal when they know that without having to speak they can communicate.

This classification appears in the first years of childhood, primarily as she continues to go to school and communicate with other children, exclusively with the infant community. These kids also have a history of anxiety in the household, becoming more vulnerable in unfamiliar circumstances to panic. The criteria for diagnosis is that for at least one month, the person exhibits symptoms, but it does not matter if it is the first month of school.

• WHAT DO TYPES OF ANXIETY HAVE THEY IN COMMON?

If you look, the forms of fear have the obsessive worry for a certain subject in general, whether it's death, being ill, because if you don't do a certain thing, something bad happens, that the snake threatens you, etc.

You live obsessed, and all your attention goes to what you are afraid of and what generally happens is that with our actions we reaffirm that it is easier to stay away or delete what we are afraid of from our lives.

They all have in common that they are both an effort to have total control over what probably happens to you in your life starting with the fact that. You claimed to be vigilant and to trigger all your senses to defend yourself, when you appeared to be disturbed by the natural world.

That is why any anxiety condition is a product of living for a long time with elevated levels of tension, and continually removing yourself from reality, of which the reality is that you are still alive and that nothing bad has happened to you (and it's not because you've stopped exposing yourself to what you are afraid of all right? It's because what you are afraid of lives in your head, not in reality).

• THE MOST POPULAR AND DANGEROUS MISTAKES THAT ANXIOUS PEOPLE MAKE

A natural and valuable emotion is fear. No, really it was evolutionarily beneficial to feel fear, as it served to ensure our longevity as a group. Therefore, if a buffalo threatened our ancestors, for instance, it was their sense of anxiety that spurred them to flee. Feeling fear helps us to respond to our environment's risks and hazards. Today, we are more likely to be inspired to reach significant goals and achieve assignments.

However, when it begins to adversely effect our day-to-day life, anxiety is not beneficial. While anxiety is difficult to get rid of, we can keep it from having a negative effect on our lives. Here are three things we can do that could make our fear stronger, really.

1. Believing everything you think.

We have thousands of everyday thoughts. Although not all of what we assume is actually true. By coming up with ideas in the form of a collection of ideas, our minds seek to make sense of the world. We should work to understand that they don't have control, rather than attempt to avoid our nervous thoughts. We will then get ourselves back to the current moment when we simply note our troubled feelings without ruminating about the past.

The more we doubt our beliefs, the easier it is to take steps that match with the beliefs (no matter what your anxious mind may be telling you).

2. Avoiding things that trigger your anxiety.

It makes sense that we should want to escape anxiety-causing circumstances, objects, and individuals. In the long run, though, this potentially creates more fear. It seems calmer now as we stop something that causes the fear. This increases the avoidant activity and as a result, you feel a good feeling.

For e.g, let's say you're nervous about going to parties. You may worry that you are going to feel insecure and that people will judge you. If you are asked to a party by a co-worker, you might find as if thinking up a reason not to go is the better choice. However, facing the things you dread repeatedly will decrease your anxiety over time. It may be good to consider working with a certified psychiatrist if you are still dealing with confronting the causes of your anxiety.

Eventually, avoiding fear-provoking conditions will take over your life and make your life very short, says Ben Rutt, Ph.D., a psychologist who specializes in anxiety. People with anxiety can stop going to public places, stop accepting further duties at work, or stop spending time with family. When I deal with an extremely insecure person, I help them eventually confront their doubts so that they can relearn what they are capable of.

3. Beating yourself up for feeling anxious.

"Laura Reagan, a licensed clinical social worker, says, "Another way to continue to stop this awkward feeling is to beat yourself up for feeling nervous. It is not helpful, because you feel bad for yourself when your inner critic pops out and berates you for your anxiety, leading to more anxiety.

For e.g., you could be tempted to say things like, "It's so stupid that I feel anxious about this." Try to treat yourself the same way you might treat a loved one who felt anxious, instead.

Psychotherapist Sarah Zalewski MS, LPC, NCC, states that it is natural to beat yourself up for feeling nervous, but "You create even more anxiety about having anxiety by concentrating on the anxiety, and your inability to deal with it."

When you are in the middle of fear, it is important that you work to be kind to yourself. Remind yourself that at this time, you are doing the best you can. Ultimately, you deserve to extend to yourself the same compassion you would offer to those you love.

You will improve your relationship with anxiety and avoid it from controlling your life by learning how to separate yourself from anxious feelings, confronting your worries, and exercising self-compassion.

4. Ruminating about who is at fault.

People also go through ruminations on who is at fault when social anxiety is caused. If someone is rude or disrespectful to you for example, and you feel offended, is it your fault to be too sensitive or the fault of the other person to be thoughtless? You could find yourself getting "shoulda, coulda" thoughts of what you should have done better to stop such a circumstance, or how you would have replied differently if only you were not in a tailspin of fear.

Instead, try to think of it like this: rumination is like turning up the temperature in a pot of water. The trap is that people who ruminate frequently do not know that they are ruminating and smart people who are particularly susceptible to this trap are used to using their thinking skills to solve problems. When it's not the correct instrument in any case, they see their rumination as problem-solving (a positive and a strength).

In addition, if you do not think it is going to work simply involving the brain with something else can serve to interrupt rumination. My colleague, Guy Winch, here discusses several techniques (like doing a Sudoku) and points out that experiments have shown how even two minutes of constructive diversion will help interrupt rumination.

5. Misinterpreting Anxiety Symptoms and stopping Medications without Supervision

The symptoms of a physical condition will resemble the signs and symptoms of an anxiety disorder.

As a result, often individuals minimize their symptoms or misunderstand them and thus avoid finding a diagnosis. Nausea, for example, may be attributed to food poisoning, but it could also be a symptom of generalized anxiety disorder (GAD). A rapid, racing heartbeat may be a symptom of a heart disease, but it also could signify a panic attack. For physical signs that recur or persist with no established underlying medical disorder, instead of attempting to self-diagnose, obtain mental health assistance.

Some individuals respond well to drugs for anti-anxiety. Others suffer side effects, which, among others, may include nausea, nightmares or joint pain. You can never avoid taking an anti-anxiety drug suddenly, though, as it may induce an anxiety disorder or cause significant signs of withdrawal. A smarter approach is to consult with the doctor monitoring the procedure about potential side effects.

You will be able to switch to another drug to receive relief from signs of anxiety without any adverse side effects.

CHAPTER 2

Irrational Behaviour Caused By Anxiety

Love is just a huge sprinkling of hormones that disrupt our usual way of acting in the brain. This can make us feel nuts, distract us and drive us crazy. All at the same moment, passion can be incredibly tiring and awesomely gorgeous. You are not able to listen to reason, logic, or follow common sense when you are irrational. You just want to satisfy a real need, whatever way that it may be.

You behave in terrific and unexpected ways before the need is met. What you must note is that not just in shaping our well-being, but also in deciding our interactions with others, feelings form an important part of our lives. Despite how hard you want to hold them in place, there are moments when negative feelings overtake you. Emotions include dynamic emotional states that influence both the body and the external world.

Your thoughts are a perception of the incidents occurring in and around you. These thoughts cause you to portray one or more behavior patterns. You get mad and can lash out when you are irritated by something or someone, and you sob when something makes you overwhelmed and sad. In the same way, you can display affection when you feel the positive emotions of love and when something is amusing, you express yourself by laughing.

A major attribute that influences your interaction with others is the ability to both understand and regulate your emotional reactions. Your relationships and even your wellbeing will be at great risk if what you do is continuously show negative feelings, also known as negative energy. In a case in which your partner does not understand why such strong emotion is needed, irrational action is a show of extreme emotion.

Romantic relationships, as well as misunderstandings often triggered by these feelings and their consequences that contribute to irrationality, are an environment where emotions run wild. The explanation for this is that certain attachment relationships are involved with them.

• BEHAVIOURS AND ANXIETY

Behaviours are an important aspect of most anxiety disorders and by necessity, to classify as an anxiety disorder, anxiety needs to affect the behavior in some way.

You do not count for a phobia, for instance, if you do not display anxiety at the sight of the phobic stimuli. If you do not get panic attacks, which are a behavioral response, you will not be eligible for panic disorder. This are all examples of ways in which fear influences behavior.

1. Mute Behaviour

Perhaps what others want to call "dejection behaviour." is the most prevalent activity. It is this necessary or the need to be alone in your feelings to attempt to deal with your anxiety."

It seems to make sense because you have anxiety. Your depression makes you feel exhausted, and you just want to be alone in order to better. Yet this is the last thing you want to do when it comes to worrying. Time spent alone without activity is time wasting on your mind, and your thoughts are your adversary in an anxiety disorder.

2. Agoraphobia

Similarly, a person may experience agoraphobia due to certain nervousness disorders, which is technically the fear of not being able to escape. Nevertheless, it normally applies to someone who refuses to abandon a position and other very special environments (such as work).

Panic illness causes agoraphobia mostly. It happens when the person starts to equate panic attacks with different locations until, eventually, more locations are synonymous with panic attacks that actually refuse to go out. Agoraphobia, considering the wide spectrum of ways anyone may be agoraphobic, is an awful condition, and one of behavior.

3. Compulsions

In all probability, the strangest actions triggered by fear are compulsions. Compulsions affect individuals with obsessive-compulsive disorder, which are activities that are compulsively carried out by a person to get rid of their anxiety-producing harmful thinking.

Compulsive actions may be linked to something. They are strongly linked to fear/obsession often. A fear of germs, for instance, may cause someone to compulsively wash their hands. Often they are connected to a desire for order, and in a particular order or sequence, an individual compulsively positions objects or things. However, in certain cases, or they may be mildly related, these illnesses may have little to do with terror at all. For instance, with;

Since you are scared a family member could be injured, they were looking for cracks in the ground.

Until you go, lock the door three times. Switch the light on and off five times, and if you are interrupted, you have to start again. These compulsions are normally twisted because the negative thinking that causes fear offers some sort of relaxation for the person. In certain situations, it might also be a coincidence, like when one day you discover that your anxious thoughts vanished when you entered from the back door, it is not obvious why these opinions or why those habits minimize them. "Different. "Different.

4. False Tools to Deal with Anxiety

False coping tools, such as substance dependence, may also be formed for people with anxiety. These kinds of habits are meant to help you deal with stress, as they minimize anxiety dramatically, so they can not annoy you as much. When you are consuming drugs or alcohol, it is hard to feel anxiety.

However, since they can intensify anxiety and create anxiety themselves, they are called false coping tools. Because of body tension and dehydration, drinking alcohol will cause strain the following day. Often a form of "use it or lose yourself" method is the ability to cope with anxiety. The more you use whiskey to help with nervousness, the more drinking is your best coping mechanism, and when you experience tension, the more your body wants.

These kinds of false coping strategies are widespread and are not confined to alcohol or medications. Any unhealthy therapeutic or physical strategy used to relieve fear is action that can cause serious coping issues in the future.

5. Nervous Tics

When they are stressed, certain individuals also experience nervous tics. Some can be rituals, like removing your nails or massaging your throat: since they are a little more in your influence, patterns are somewhat different from spasms, but otherwise, when you feel anxious, they are involuntary.

A medical mystery is nervous tics. No one is aware why it happens or why it affects others, but not others, or what actually causes it and why it arises, but in people with anxiety disorders, tics and nervous behaviors are very normal.

6. Anxiety Behaviours

It is therefore important to note that physical behaviour is not the only mode of practice. With anxiety, thinking practices are common, including things such as:

• Generalized Anxiety Disorder

This form of anxiety characterizes persistent and excessive problems that are difficult to manage. The topic is rather complex, because a person with generalized anxiety will think about something and experience persistent fears. It is also not strange that the person encounters anxiety effects without understanding exactly why.

It influences well-being and can interfere with day-to-day routines, when they have a persistent fear that at some moment something bad will happen. For instance, a person with generalized anxiety will spend the entire day imagining that while she is driving; her companion will have a traffic accident and will carry out the action of repeatedly contacting her to figure out if she is okay. In addition, the condition must be satisfied by the requirement that it must take place on most days for a minimum duration of 6 months.

• Medication / Substance Anxiety Disorder

There is evidence in a situation that signs of anxiety or panic attacks have occurred immediately after or after a time of opioid intoxication or withdrawal. Alternatively, to take a drug that is capable of generating these answers.

- Anxiety disorder due to medical illness
- Anxiety or panic attack is due to the direct physiological aspects of other medical conditions.
- Other specified / unspecified anxiety disorders
- Anxiety disorders with clinically significant symptoms are included here but do not meet all the diagnostic criteria for any of the diseases outlined above.

You should state the explanation why the conditions do not satisfy (for example, that the situation does not last for the time set), because because of a lack of knowledge, certain requirements may not be in the decision. In the other hand, in addition to the criteria we have addressed, the ICD-10 (International Classification of Diseases) adds:

• Mixed Anxiety-Depressive Disorder

The anxiety-depressive disorder Combined happens where both anxiety and depression-related symptoms arise, but neither prevails over the other, or illnesses are serious enough to be independently diagnosed. It is a chronic illness that is associated with sick leave or academic leave, but they are the ones who least call for psychiatric support, being much milder than most conditions.

It should last longer than a month and should not be connected to very difficult and critical incidents in life (but would fall into the category of adjustment disorders).

Other mixed anxiety disorders

For starters, obsessive-compulsive disorder, dissociative disorders (such as dissociative fugue), somatization disorders, undifferentiated somatoform disorder, and hypochondriac disorder were originally fear disorders throughout earlier iterations of the DSM. They have been extracted from this group in the most recent edition, but there is no doubt that anxiety plays an important role in these circumstances.

1. Sleep Disorders

Technically, they are all habits. Anxiety itself in a sense is a behavioral problem. When there is no terror, it is the beginning of the fight or flight reaction. It is not rare to see several different kinds of behaviors and peculiar signs that occur as a result after activation.

That is why taking action to monitor, monitor, and heal your fear is the best way to avoid these habits.

• HOW TO STOP THESE BEHAVIOURS

Learning to "switch" thoughts

1. Focus of Attention

It reveals everything that happens around us, everything we take on trust or sense, which has meaning for us this, is our interpretation, what we call knowledge, or the sum of ideas about truth.

Since infancy, the vision of the future has been in the making, and it details in depth what is possible for us in this life and what is not. Based on the image of the people around him a child's image is formed - parents, classmates, teachers, etc. In addition, he goes through life with this card.

This map expands with the passing of time and the emergence of new perspectives. Even the entire paradox is that from experience, a person perceives all subsequent events; it is very hard to go beyond. The universe is composed of ideas and is in the subconscious. "Any picture of the world with a constant focus on it "comes to life.

Scrolling to yourself or your loved ones through terror in your mind is hopeless - the force of panic will only aggravate the situation. What we think about is found most often in our lives. Changing your views, you start to act differently and accomplish multiple outcomes. The idea that making your own experiences is under your hands, and not just adapting to external situations or memories of the past, suggests that you have a large choice, the freedom to control your life and develop your future.

Hence, changing the focus of your mind in a constructive direction is an ideal way to get rid of anxiety.

2. Exclude Lousy News from Your Life Whenever Possible

Do not watch or read news about violence, accounts of earthquakes and conflicts, so you provide an opportunity for anxiety, to sink into the negative. Turn off your TV and miss articles on this topic. There is no benefit from this data, but your sensitivity is starting to draw scary images. For yourself, build a positive knowledge field, emphasis on the positive side of life.

3. Cross out the Negative from Your Life

Profitable exchange

The appearance of fear mainly offers the imagination of an individual, the ability to associate. The invention draws images of a terrible future when you worry.

The paintings can be huge and stand all the time in front of your eyes. However, what if a pleasant one substitutes an unpleasant image?

Imagine a situation that brings you memories that are pleasant. Determine how you feel by vividly imagining this joyful experience. Next, let the image come closer to you so that vibrant colors become more important, brighter, and take on it. Pay attention once again to your feelings. Did they change? Perhaps they have become stronger?

Let the images pass away now get smaller, sketchier, weaker, to almost the size of a postage stamp shrinks. What thoughts do you have now?

Send the picture back to its original location after deciding this. This occurs for most people: as a good event arrives - positive emotions increase, and as it goes on - they diminish significantly. Simply put them closer to the eyes of the mind if you want to feel optimistic thoughts more intensively. However, if you wish to have less stressful encounters, you will drive them away from you.

You may also deal with a state of fear, driving far far from negative thoughts, or turning them into a point that is hardly visible.

CHAPTER 3

Jealousy in a Relationship

Jealousy refers to the risk of losing a partner, of being tricked or discarded by a partner, of being replaced by someone else. The "Jealousy" reaction is characterized by skewed and unfounded feelings about our partner and our relationship, which creates apprehension and anxiety reactions, and behaviour to exert control over the activities of the pair, to seek protection and alleviate our concerns.

In this way, we are not referring to an "illness" when we talk of envy (although it often seems profoundly ingrained and uncontrollable like the person), but rather a way of handling the relationship that has been well read. We refer to a behavioral trend that (as it translates into a series of thoughts and behaviours). It means that we should learn to modify this detrimental way of treating the relationship when an envy issue is found.

A prevalent phenomenon is jealousy in relationships. Naturally, when a loved one does not believe you or is wary of you and your climate, this is an uncomfortable feeling. This behaviour will trigger serious issues with relationships. If you are operating on faith, though, then you will conquer envy.

Although we are all jealous from time to time. However, in a relationship, so much and unavoidable envy can be very counterproductive to your union and can save you from enjoyment in life. How can you say if your friendship has so much protectiveness? Unhealthy and pathological envy is demonstrated by strong signals.

• **How to Identify Jealousy?**

- Your partner wants you to be his only
- Control of behaviour
- Accusations without evidence
- The manifestation of mistrust
- Constant calls and a desire to know where you are
- Emotional and physical abuse
- You are always under observation by someone.
- What causes excessive jealousy?
- How to respond to jealousy in a relationship?
- How to cope with jealousy?
- Remember that your partner chose you and not someone else
- Work on your self-esteem
- Try to be more gullible

1. Your Partner Wants You to Be His Only

A jealous spouse wants to separate you as much as he can from other people. When you share time with other people, even though it is your own family, he never enjoys it. He wants to separate you as much as he can from people close to you and he sees other people as a danger to your friendship. He is simply not self-confident and worries that you might be closer to other people than to him.

2. Control of Behaviour

This is a major sign of possessiveness and excessive envy if your loved one tries to dictate how you look, with whom you relax, how you spend your money, and how you act in general. It is very easy to spot these individuals. However, often men and women who are in a relationship, for one reason or another, resign themselves to such conduct.

3. Accusations without Evidence

Even if there is no proof of this, a jealous lover will still find a justification to suspect you of deceit or infidelity. In addition, when you remember that you have not done enough to merit these fines, it is very disappointing.

4. The Manifestation of Mistrust

You may often find that your companion scans your computer, logs into your social network accounts and instant messengers without your consent. It scans the emails and looks at phone calls. A strong indication of the problems of envy, mistrust, and power is this action.

5. Constant Calls and a Desire to Know Where You Are

He/she will want to constantly and frequently interact with you and find out what you are doing. It is because a person needs to control everything because he acts as if he wants to check you out because he wants to make sure you do not spend time with other men or women.

6. Emotional and Physical Abuse

Jealous and possessive persons display verbal and physical insults very frequently. They make you feel guilty, accuse you without evidence, and do not give you enough room and personal time.

7. You Are Always Under Observation

Have you ever found that your companion emerges anywhere, wherever you are, or at certain moments when you encounter friends, supposedly coincidentally? Perhaps by sending someone to flirt with you just to see if you are going to react, he/she tests your loyalty. An unhealthy mentality represents unhealthy jealousy in relationships.

- **WHAT CAUSES EXCESSIVE JEALOUSY?**

In partnerships, several factors can trigger mistrust. The most common explanation is that an individual has attributes that influence and abuse (as in many cases of domestic violence). The worse appears to be this sort of envy. That it requires abusive, behavioural control, and potentially life-threatening conditions.

• WHAT IT IS

Jealousy, in one way or another, ends up appearing in every relationship. This feeling is part of our relations, and while it is always painful for us to embrace it whether we often repress it, it causes more severe pain. It is important to take care not to associate envy with the sensation of love or intimacy as they arise in the pair, because this emotion has nothing to do with this.

In relationships, jealousy is one of the most important causes of dispute. That is because of the sense of possession we have which is part of our history. They remind us of a significant truth, assuming that the other person may be lost.

This condition alerts us to the possibility of missing the love and devotion that our companion gives us for another person's benefit.

Both our doubts, our shortcomings, and the challenges we have not been able to solve are reflected in a couple of relationships. In all their repertoire of interactions and learning to place them in common, two people meet. When relationships between people are still complex, they are more complicated for the pair. Intimacy is revealed, and then the other party is vulnerable to us.

Ideas, behaviours and separate motives collide with each other in coexistence. Without a question, it is an outstanding test to understand the importance the other party has for us to find agreement and mutual well-being. It is important to give in collectively, rather than for ourselves, to search for the couple. Some variables are essential foundations for improving the relationship and for preserving it over time. Trust and respect stand out between them. These two basic components allow envy not to become a cause of everlasting disputes in which pain is permanent.

• What does jealousy entail in the relationship?

Have you ever felt the envy towards your mate was a demonstration of love? You have to know, if so, that this is a major mistake. Jealousy is never a feature of passion. Jealousy, instead of fear, is a symptom of uneasiness and lack of bond reinforcing. They still have a lot to do with the person who encounters them, when they can have a wrong moment in the relationship and seem more insecure.

It may also state that there is legitimate jealousy in which the other party gives up, does not pay attention or does such actions in the relationship that are not spoken, agreed upon or permitted by the two partners.

Relationship envy is an ideal source of data and it can supply us with precious signals. These are some of the most common cases, depending on what circumstances exist, severity and frequency.

• Lack of Communication and Intimacy

Fewer memories are exchanged as the bond breaks, and people are estranged, and it is easy for envy to surface on one side of the other, or both.

• Possessive and Dependent Character

There are human personalities that are more jealous than most, and the more anxious with what their mate might be doing with other people are the people who are more lacking and inattentive. They would assume that they are not good enough or valuable enough for their relationship if they already have poor self-esteem. These individuals have a greater propensity to be possessive and reliant if they fail to settle their disputes.

• Indifference and Lack of Motivation

It is an outstanding indicator of the crisis, and the connection is deteriorating. In addition, if there is no desire or inspiration left, it is time to reflect about what is happening and about a potential breakup. The other appears to assume that something happens to one of the individuals because it is because other individuals are involved, which ends up being envy.

Maybe everything about your relationship is stopping functioning, and that's what you need to be part of. You have to look into why you see what can be solved and what is a part of you as mistrust emerges. Enable contact, above all not to imagine much of what is going on and make it transparent. It's the only way to determine whether what's going on is part of you how you feel, is indicative of a deterioration of your partner's partnership, or whether your partner has chosen to leave the relationship, and the signs are obvious and noticeable. The courses of action are distinct in each situation.

• JEALOUSY IN PSYCHOLOGY

In psychology, jealousy is a dominant emotion inherent in many individuals who stick to conventional family values. Some claim that a strong sense of possessiveness is a direct proof of affection, while others believe that it is incredibly dangerous and that the most successful alliances are broken. The statement that envy itself does not have a positive or negative vector is closer to the facts. The more rational solution would be not to ignore the blatant signs of cheating and not to torment the partner with persistent complaints and false claims at the same time.

Jealousy is an emotion that can naturally flow against the individual's own will or occur for one of the many causes that will be used in the comprehensive discussion below. If you dig a little closer, because of the subject's ability to regulate several life cycles that are not based on his will, a heightened sense of ownership emerges. A spouse may be infuriated by extreme interpersonal interactions, which involve the most unexpected consequences. Therefore, a couple with confidence issues can take a consultation with a qualified counselor.

In both children and pets, envy is inherent, because a sense of possession is not a disease. It is all about the severity of the experience, and in the case of poisoning others' lives, it is necessary to take action to get rid of them as quickly as possible. In adults, where do the prerequisites for envy come from? Psychologists suggest that in persons who have not gained affection, love, and parental care in infancy, intense destructive feelings frequently emerge.

• WHY PEOPLE ARE JEALOUS

Jealousy in the area of couple of relationships is feelings of fear and anguish that, when there are a variety of circumstances, invade either or both members of a sentimental spouse. This negative feeling will emerge when they believe as if the other's love is in danger, or when they realize with anxiety that they avoid being the loved one's center of focus.

• Jealousy in a Relationship

It is also said that, without jealousy, there is no love. Also studies carried out in the United States suggests that marriages in which couples are jealous of each other last longer than those in which there is no suspicion or may not manifest too much. Will the right emotion still have to make room for a touch of envy? A friendship is cemented by healthy distrust, and it is an indication that the couples care for each other. The dilemma occurs when jealousy takes on an unhealthy dimension, because when the partner is regulated, the life of two individuals is warning. Slowly, the relationship continues to imitate life in a prison, and there is a loss of breath, dignity, and liberty. Jealousy is not equivalent to jealousy, as you can see.

• What Is Behind the Jealousy?

As several songs suggest, the origin of envy is not love, but fear: the fear of losing what we have, or that we believe in the right to own.

• Reasons for Jealousy of a Partner

What is envy? This feeling is characterized by psychologists as frustration and fear of a partner's future loss, as a sense of distress resulting from the real or imagined relationship between the spouse and a third party. It is this assumption that someone else might be more desirable to the spouse than ourselves, creating certain unpleasant feelings, such as grief, remorse, anger, a sense of deprivation, and moving into the need to dominate the life of our chosen heart. There are also damaging habits, such as showing messages sent to the mailbox of the partner, tracking SMSs sent to her spouse, wondering what the partner did all day long, who he met, etc. It is not possible to mistake jealousy with caution. Morbid jealousy means that the partner loses trust.

It is difficult to avoid quarrels and minor quarrels in a partnership with another partner. You are not going to go ahead of them.

Why are people jealous of their partners? There are several explanations. Typically, outside of themselves, causes of envy are seen, e.g., through the aggressive behavior of a partner that catches the interest of possible rivals. More commonly, however the motivations of envy are caught in ourselves and include, among other things:

Jealousy is caused by many causes; they may happen together or in isolation.

• Fear of Being Alone

It makes us afraid to know that we are not irreplaceable, afraid of the loss of the person we share our lives with. We feel we are going to be isolated after missing it and we are not going to meet someone like him/her or that they are not going to love us as he/she does. Then there are feelings of vulnerability and desperation, which cause mistrust in any circumstance we perceive to be a danger that might bring us closer to that isolation. Thus, jealousy emerged.

• Low Self-esteem

The profile of the jealous is connected to the lack of trust and fear towards oneself. Sometimes, vulnerable individuals do not feel capable of their partner's affection and therefore appear to be wary of it. They are afraid to encounter another person who might be more intelligent, beautiful, or compassionate to find out how little it is worth. Poor self-esteem expresses itself in contrasts with oneself, rivalry with others and the fear of replacement. This is typically the most common scenario, but often the jealous person will not understand low self-esteem, nor will he feel associated with these lines.

• Life Experiences

It is more likely that people who have ever been deceived by someone they admired would later grow a jealous attitude. Friends, relatives, old relationships, or the same friendship that has had ups and downs that are impossible to forget, would make the entity worry and behave jealously over the same thing that might happen to him as in the past.

• FEMININE AND MASCULINE JEALOUSY

Through their feelings of envy, women and men vary. Women most often envy the energy and time committed by the partner to other women (emotional betrayal), whereas men react more strongly to sexual betrayal. You just do not want to invest in a kid of yours. Women often worry more frequently, about whether a partner would cheat on them (unsatisfied sexual needs, more attractive rival, lack of passion, etc.). The reasons that their mate is sexually involved in alternative relationships are impossible to be analyzed by men. Men and women view jealousy differently. In women, grief and despair arise, and in males, frustration and violence. More frequently, men deny that they are jealous. On the other hand, women are most frequently the party that initiates jealousy to verify a relationship's durability and the level of love that binds couples.

Jealousy, if dosed in the correct amounts, will improve a friendship. It destroys love and faith when it is too much and too heavy. The partner might feel cornered, not be able to tolerate relentless influence, and just leave the relationship exhausted.

• Psychological disorders

Narcissistic, paranoid, and histrionic traits have a clear inclination to mistrust people and thus to constantly cultivate envy. Other personalities also experience this condition, owing to their weakness.

Calotype is a psychopathology that has, without any logical argument or evidence of the truth that proves it a mistaken belief as its core axis. These individuals experience such strong feelings of envy that they are the focus of their lives, their way of thought and behaving. In addition to taking acts such as limiting the freedom of movement and expression of the other person, stalking them, investigating them, and often attacking them, they also clash with their partner. Many offer love as the ideal justification to defend their abuse, but one thing must be clear: there is no love for jealousy.

To be diagnosed as a calotype, the symptoms of a person with this condition must last at least a month and while it is typically a recurrent disorder, oscillations in the severity of delusional thoughts occur.

• Consequences of Irrational Jealousy

Sometimes, married spouses confuse envy as affection. Yet passion is not at all a product of abnormal envy. If anger is unnoticed, so as a jealous person gets more and more afraid, furious, and dominant, it can destroy the relationship over time.

This emotion produces a self-fulfilling prophecy for those with abnormal envy. As couples attempt to discourage them, their deepest fears of losing love and affection are fulfilled, says Robert L. Barker in The Green-Eyed Marriage.

Jealousy will lead to anger and self-defense in the end. It can also undermine confidence in relationships and lead to more disagreements, especially if a jealous individual makes demands and constantly asks other people questions.

Intense interpersonal responses can also contribute to physical signals. Jealous people also deal with emotional responses, such as shaking, dizziness, exhaustion, and sleeping issues. Their constant rage and desire for support may also lead to the end of a friendship or marriage, especially if they become cruel and do not cope in healthy ways with their envy.

• How to Deal with Protectiveness in Relationship

If your relationship is suffering from envy problems, before they get out of control, it is important to fix them. Here are some Healthy Envy Ideas.

• Understand That Jealousy Is Normal

There will be persons and situations that endanger your wedding's protection. If it's a flirtatious employee or a job that needs a lot of travel, having a little envy is very reasonable. You need to take the time to resolve your concerns and settle on some limitations that will secure your marriage and your hearts.

For instance, you will both accept that it is necessary to limit interaction with a flirty colleague for the wellbeing of the marriage. Alternatively, you can conclude that distress may be relieved by a bedtime discussion when one of the partners is on the drive. The primary thing is that you address matters peacefully and come up with ideas together.

• Get to the Roots of Jealousy

When one of the couples experiences envy on an ongoing basis, it is important to figure out why this happens. For instance, does a jealous partner feel insecure because as a couple, you do not spend much time together? On the other hand, does marriage have trouble with faith due to infidelity? Ask questions, instead of defending yourself or resenting envy. In order to relieve it, strive to grasp where jealousy comes from and what can be achieved.

• Create an Atmosphere of Trust

The development of a troposphere of faith is one of the easiest ways to defend yourself from envy. For both friends being trustworthy, this process continues. They are in other words, real, loyal, and trustworthy. Credible individuals are not dishonest about how they spend their time. They do not cheat on their partners either. If you are mindful of these pitfalls together, confidence in collaborations will expand and supplant envy.

• Develop Healthy Attachment

Seeking opportunities to share time to get close together. Marriage is more than simply living together and sharing a bed together. This entails the manifestation of attachment, sharing time together and developing an attachment to one another. In addition, any threat to your love can be a source of fear. Jealousy, where it is an indicator that marriage is at risk, is acceptable.

• Recognize When Jealousy Offends

Jealousy is healthy in a relationship. Although it could be a red flag if one of the couples were jealous for no reason. Particularly if intense frustration, unreasonable expectations, and false claims are involved in suspicion. This sort of envy however is not a one-time occurrence. A behavioral trend repeats repeatedly. Another indication of offensive or unhealthy envy is the effort, as well as outlandish charges, to establish control over another individual. If you realize that you are reacting to the questions, "I was only" or I was just ..." this is a red flag. Before anything gets out of control, you need to find assistance urgently.

• Cope with Your Jealousy

If you are the one in your relationship who battles jealousy, you might wonder about why you feel jealous. Are you dealing with self-esteem, for instance, or are you scared your wife will abandon you? Or maybe in the past your partner was mistaken, and you are concerned that this is going to happen again?

Your jealous emotions need to be pushed back out in any situation. Finding a psychologist or psychotherapist who can help you learn how to handle your jealousy in safe ways is the perfect way to do this.

Jealousy, if properly treated, may be a motivation for development, as most other dynamic emotional interactions. For both you and your partner, turning to anger will be the first path to growing self-awareness and deeper comprehension. To conquer your jealous feelings, here are several moves.

- Admit you're jealous
- Recognize your envy is damaging your marriage
- Discuss your jealous thoughts' origins
- Accept that the partner should not be spied on
- Deciding to change your actions
- Know that not anyone else can be managed; however, you can handle your response.

- Establish fair ground rules that can be agreed by all of you to
- Request expert assistance as a married couple, if possible.

CHAPTER FOUR

Understand the Fear of Loneliness and Rules for a Happy and Relationship

Fear is an emotion, which is required. It has enabled us to be alert from the beginning of our life, to measure danger, to protect ourselves, and to be safe, to make it normal and useful. At present, it only serves the same role in conditions other than those of millions of years ago. Yet, on several occasions, there are risks that definitely are not true, which we call unreasonable fear.

Our genus is a gregarious and social being so we prefer to be related to other individuals naturally. Nevertheless, as it becomes a dependence, it becomes a challenge and we resist learning how to be alone, causing anxiety and actions to attempt and prevent being alone.

Loneliness is a situation or feeling that at some time of our lives we have been through or may go through. We will have to be alone sometimes, but it is far from constantly feeling alone. There are very different reasons why we can feel alone: for being excluded, for believing, as we do not fit in for dying, etc.

In the last two decades, solitude has been a recurrent theme.

A modern trend emerged in the vacuum left behind by the gods that once legitimized human relationships and practices. That barren, cold and pointless area of human isolation is created by the distance between individuals. The most conducive ground for human compromise and shame is the fear of isolation that has recently arisen in its sick ways. We miss our lives with the same care, enjoy the shadows of others and prefer outer orbits.

Fear of isolation throws us before the sight of an inner nothingness that emerged against the backdrop of any initial discoveries being overlooked. Although we have a commercial motto, "we are born alone and die alone," we are spending a great deal of our money to escape this sad scenario.

• BEING ALONE IS A FAILURE; FEELING ALONE IS A HUMILIATION

We have our isolation that everyone knows about and public loneliness that only we know about by handling our loneliness in compartments every day. A social life full of failed attempts to crack our cocoon reveals the landscape thereby formed. Working experience of colleagues with whom we emulate the illusion of communion and being at home, where we unexpectedly wake up alone in vacuum, freezing and abandoned from its living periphery, returning in the evening and discovering the dead internet link.

All of life seems like a sport at the blurred end of lucidity in which we build sandcastles around our isolation. Loneliness, on the other hand, is an error in interpretation, we are imbued with the existence of others, and though we weep alone under the duvet, we are linked to this world.

• Eremophobia or Phobia of Loneliness

We may be referring to various places when we speak about isolation, such as fear of not having a girlfriend, fear of getting older, fear of being friendly, fear of rejection from others and fear of spending time by myself alone.

Therefore, isolation is an unfounded anxiety that being lonely does not pose any immediate threat to anyone, although certain persons will often create a lock that is disabling.

When we speak about eremophobia or isolation phobia, we apply to individuals that might experience irrational dislike or distress, and who are directly disproportionate to the thought of becoming isolated, often for limited periods, and can end up suffering from hallucinations or panic attacks, even with clinical signs of extreme anxiety.

As social species, human beings continuously require intimate interactions with others to feel loved, not the contact that we deem fundamental with a single individual entity. That is why we claim loneliness is a true fear because the person can face it, but it is not a reasonable fear because in these circumstances there are no reasons to be afraid.

It is important to be mindful that it is an unfounded concern when we are afraid of isolation, which is very widespread. It is not fair because for instance, despite being alone at home for a weekend, we are not going to lose an arm, an eye, or life; there is no need to be objectively frightened. It stems from feelings and an inner conversation in which we convince ourselves that isolation is a bad thing and that we have to be scared of that fear of loneliness because of those thoughts we feel. For example, the fear of becoming alone, having been through a breakup; it is not true isolation because we are not alone this sort of fear of loneliness can also sound ridiculous.

At least once in his life, each person developed a fear of isolation. Many people recognize that loneliness is not a word, and much of it relies on itself whether there is an effort to improve the situation. To find friends or your individual, for example, who will brighten up daily life and share days of joy? This terror though will restrict the will of even the friendliest personalities, surrounded by a large number of individuals. Then the person has ideas on what you need to do about it. So there is what here?

One of the most prevalent and serious phobias of our day is the fear of isolation, which carries with it many issues, including psycho-emotional addictions, psychosomatic disorders, panic assaults. Fear of isolation also drives a person to where he does not want to be.

A number of meanings of this definition by various scholars are correlated with the issue of evaluating loneliness: a feeling of loneliness and social exclusion, traumatic memories of involuntary separation, and voluntary loneliness associated with existential search. The sense of loneliness carries out a regulating role and is incorporated into the feedback system that enables the individual to monitor the optimum level of interpersonal contacts. Nevertheless, a person's physical solitude does not necessarily translate to alienation.

A young man or woman who is unable to find a compatible

spouse or an older parent, lost friends and loved ones, and unable to find a shared language with the younger generation, may experience loneliness. People with an inert nervous system also feel isolation, failing to communicate with new contacts, eventually getting used to new friends. Isolation may contribute to depression in severe cases.

Reminiscent of isolation, but at the same time, because of a circumstance, or disposition (psychological type) of the person, do not wear such a deep character, lack of contact of input. The cause of isolation, in particular, may be fundamental pathological changes in the individual's psyche.

Some psychological causes lead to loneliness. For instance, it may be low self-esteem, which leads to the avoidance of contact with other people - for fear of being exposed to scrutiny, which in fact, causes a vicious spiral because of the loss of self-esteem in contact declines lower. Weak coping skills tend to loneliness as well. People with poorly developed interpersonal communication skills, low socialization, fear that they will suffer a relationship breakdown or get into psychological dependency, and therefore prefer to be isolated, particularly if they already have a bad history of interacting with others. In music, cinema, literature and poetry, loneliness as a state is usually oral.

• TYPES OF FEAR OF LONELINESS

A dilemma that may be extreme is isolation. Many other challenges, such as the loss of social networks provided by society and the acceptance of unhealthy habits, are believed to go hand in hand. Fear is a distressing feeling induced by the appearance of threat that is actual or perceived.

It is a response that starts with a painful stimulus and ends with the release of chemicals that cause the heart and lungs to speed up or the body to become nervous, among other things. Fear also triggers reactions that are characteristic of the response to stress, and reaction is known as a response to fight or flight.

This is a difficult process, though, which does not necessarily present itself in exactly the same manner, nor does it have the same sources. That is why we are concerned about the kind of anxiety of being alone.

• The Main Types of Loneliness

It is a description of the kinds of isolation that we may experience in our lives. These are of course, not mutually high-class groups, so some can overlap.

1. Contextual Loneliness

Loneliness does not necessarily apply to all spheres of life; it is part of a single sense often.

For example, even though he feels connected too many loved ones elsewhere, someone who has no friends or associates at the college where he takes classes or at work can experience isolation there.

2. Transitory Loneliness

When examining the forms of isolation that people feel, it is crucial to understand the time factor. It occurs in particular cases in the case of transitory, which does not last much longer than a day.

For example, when a disagreement arises in a relationship of love or affection, the impression may emerge that there is an obstacle that divides us from the other, or that a facet of his personality has been exposed to us that, if we realize it, makes us reconsider.

3. Chronic Loneliness

This type of isolation is not based on a single context or situation, but is perpetuated over time remaining in various areas of the life of an individual. Of course, it does not mean that it can never die or that we can't do anything to make it disappear; it will weaken before it leaves, under the right circumstances, but this costs more than in other more detailed classes of isolation.

It must be borne in mind, on the other hand, that the distinction between persistent and transitory isolation is just a matter of degree, and that there is no direct distinction between them.

So for instance, we can find instances in which an entity is exposed to an incredibly monotonous life that only consists of one kind of atmosphere and feels lonely. In this situation, whether it were persistent or transitory, it will not be clear because we can recognize that it has been static in a moment of its existence that repeats itself day after day over and over again.

4. Self-imposed Loneliness

There are situations in which solitude is the value of alienation that you have opted to use as a distinguishing feature in your own life, such as individuals that are fearful of becoming frustrated by friends or their loved ones, and who grow misanthropic behaviors or distrust towards people in general.

In certain instances, for religious purposes, such as the will to consecrate oneself to a life of devotion to one or more gods, this type of loneliness may also occur, without thus accepting feelings of animosity towards other people.

5. Loneliness Imposed

The solitude placed is the result, against the latter's will of a series of material deprivations to which the person is subjected. The failure to have frequent and prolonged relationships adds to the appearance of a sense of loneliness, a sensation that correlates to empirical truth, such as the loss of free time or the experience of living and rarely leaving a small location.

In the other hand, the fact that another enforces isolation does not mean that the being of that meaning is the purpose of the interventions imposed on those who experience it. It can be activated, for instance, by very stressful working hours, in which making money is the main thing.

6. Existential Loneliness

Existential alienation is somewhat different from other forms of solitude because the frequency and amount of experiences we have with other people has relatively little impact. Alternatively, it is a situation in which the sense of alienation blends with the existential doubt of what one exists for and what binds us to another specifically.

If self-awareness is a subjective, private reality that can not be communicated, it can be clear that our life is profoundly different from our world and those that occupy it.

The loss of sense for life itself, on the other hand, will lead to make us feel detached from the rest of the universe. That is to say, it is an environment that causes frustration or concern in general, and that can not be resolved by seeking to make more friends or encounter more individuals.

• TYPES OF PSYCHOLOGICAL FEAR OF LONELINESS.

7. Objective loneliness

The social stigma attached to isolation is such as inducing certain individuals to make pleasant or romantic choices that are unsatisfactory or unsatisfactory, only to gain a place in the ranks of not alone.'

Paradoxically, the fear of being alone, often unintentionally, or wasting time in one's exclusive business, will plunge all life into the limbo of overcrowding interpersonal replacements, overflowing solitude with pseudo-friends and pseudo-love, with the single superstitious goal of escaping vituperated alienation.

In this way, another problem is created and nurtured to overcome the problem of true isolation: subjective loneliness.

When you are in the middle of strangers, friends, or a companion, you are subjectively lonely, feeling a general frustration, having a peculiar uneasiness, near to tears. That is as, when repetition and everyday life pursue each other without pleasure; our social world starts to exist as a poorly planned collage on the continuous level of intolerance, boredom, and fantasy.

8. Subjective Loneliness

Subjective loneliness is a deeper and barren land of solitude, illustrating that despite itself in the course of life, migrants or refugees traveling away from their countries have misplaced the affections, as in the case of grieving or briefly.

The latter survive a scenario and, while they can adapt and then travel in search of someone who can improve their circumstance with considerable difficulties. In the other side, in an active portion, which is subjectively lonely and responsible for a tangle of overt relationships, fake relationships and nostalgic camouflage of which that person ends up feeling like a hostage between courses and appeals and in which he continues to recognise the only emotional references possible.

His world is centered on social networks. The misuse of social networks and chats, where real relational cemeteries are created, with a virtual place and a picture for each instrument whose usage can be inversely proportional to the validity of the person and their relationships, is a blinding representation of subjective isolation.

As a result, even though Facebook, they prefer to prolong fiction and launch an impression of themselves pursuing the framework under which they view themselves as alien, exhausted, and misunderstood in fact. Nothing is more alienating than simulating engagement, displaying esteem, and influencing an interpersonal resonance for those who eventually disregard our tremendous alienation.

9. A Third Loneliness

There is a third sense of isolation, that for a certain time of his life, someone who does not deny or hide his personality and dignity and lives. Between himself and others and he gives himself the privilege of enjoying himself in the very presence of his being almost entirely.

Others develop their identity, are acquainted with internal inconsistencies, contend with the anxiety of being isolated, question social alienation tabulation.

As a way of being surrounded by something they want, enticing them and making them feel content, they prefer isolation. Such persons do not need to conform with the practices learned in society, which involve mates, husbands, mothers, children, whoever they may be to prevent being alone." at all times.

A cathartic moment will reflect this third loneliness about rational and subjective solitude, creating a self-consciousness capable of triggering new emotional processes, selectively, a social life that is eventually fulfilling.

A state of arranging our lives and relationships to know how to abandon those that, while unwittingly, attach and depress us and dedicate ourselves to dissolve the chain of negative perceptions and senses is a condition that satisfies this distinct, somewhat doubtful view of oneself throughout the world.

WHY THIS HAPPENS

We may all come to believe as if no one is capable of recognizing us that we remain confused no matter how well we communicate our feelings. That as a side effect brings with it a relentless feeling of isolation. In comparison, depression takes on certain aspects more often in the case of women; conventional gender stereotypes can contribute to certain kinds of isolation.

It is also normal to hear the traditional expression "I feel alone," while people may surround this girl. The feeling of loneliness is irrational and does not respond to incidents when they unfold, but is a contextual feeling instead. We can see how to handle these conditions in this report.

• WHY DOES THIS FEELING OF LONELINESS APPEAR?

1. Childhood Problems

Often there are moments in life that a child feels misled by people close to him. If parents are distracted with the equipment of their personal lives or job development to the detriment of their child's education, I happen. Dads and mothers who are too busy most much send their children to friends, and wealthy families have nannies. The relocation of one of the parents to another family is often a major loss for a baby or teenager.

This fact is highly compounded by the resulting presence of a half-brother or sister, which does not often appease an offended child. Even a seemingly harmless expression such as don't calm down I'll give you to another aunt (uncle)" will cause a baby's system of auto phobia (fear of loneliness). A self-contained person in the future is an outcome,

2. Low Self-esteem

Just those individuals who do not tear themselves away from the mirror at the sight of a beautiful reflection in it live long. The fear of being lonely is not understood to egoists and daffodils, so they feel good about themselves in a beautiful company. There are very few such persons, though because all such celebrities require others to respect them. In the case of low self-esteem, a person starts to fear that those around him will notice his shortcomings and abandon him.

3. Personal Stagnation

Worrying that personal projects have not been completed is often a cause that drives individuals to feel isolated. Social stigmas that impair the tranquility of many individuals are usually not properly achieved in their age or a stable partner. In certain situations, there is a desperate need to meet someone special only for this purpose.

4. Superficial Relationships

The feeling of isolation will soon come when our relationships of friendship are not essential, and now are based more on the superficial. We must always share our thoughts and listen to what our loyal friends have to say.

5. Grief Process

A loved one's absence will trigger feelings of isolation, whether it is due to death or because you have moved to another country. Feeling the important person's absence will carry the feeling that we have been left behind imminently.

6. Too Much Work

There is no spare time if much of your life revolves around work (paid or unpaid), and quality relationships with other individuals can hardly be formed. This is a challenge, given that many women have to dedicate their energies to both cultivating a professional career and devoting themselves to most household jobs.

7. Inability to Trust

If a person were marked by intense distrust, so learning how to develop friendships would be even tougher for her a fear of relationships exists. The failure to trust influences the understanding of the surrounding reality and the people around it significantly. When there is an opportunity to face failure or some other negative circumstance again, anxiety emerges. It is difficult for a person immersed in depressive emotions to feel very happy and prosperous. It constantly seems to him that he is awaited only by trouble.

8. Psychological Trauma

As a product of traumatic distress, anxiety also occurs. In addition, it does not matter how effective the expression is. Maybe the key thing is that the personal value system is evolving. An assumption of the worst-case situation occurs. If a person does not understand how to get out of this authoritarian society, so it will appear to him that no one can assist him. Therefore, there is an alienation curtain, which makes it difficult to glance sideways at the case. Despair and emptiness in the soul will permanently settle the existence of psychological distress.

- **15 GOLDEN RULES FOR A HAPPY AND LASTING RELATIONSHIP**

Relationships are as plain as you find them, or as nuanced. In the beginning, couples that were very much in love can break up, and couples whom part ways may get back together. There are two parties behind any good relationship who put in endless time and effort; but some couples make it seem effortless.

1. Know why you love your partner

Due to their intellect, beauty, or something else, you may have fallen in love with your mate. However, when you start staying with them, you find that they have a bad temper, that they are sloppy with their things, or that they snore while asleep. These insignificant items can contribute to conflict. The best advice for relationships is to be true to yourself on whether you like your mate, understand their strong points, and consider their shortcomings. Occasionally, it is okay to wonder whether you did the right thing to choose this person, but this feeling is only short lived if your love is real.

2. Know their needs and fulfill them

Your mate may not articulate it, but they may have such expectations of you. When they are unwell, they might ask you to take care of them, talk to them when they feel sad, or support them out financially when the need arises. This is a two-way thing, part of being in a relationship wants to consider the desires of your partner, and it is the obligation of everyone to express their needs and to strive to try to satisfy them as long as both of your aspirations are reasonable.

3. Have realistic expectations

You may dream of a knight in shining armor or a princess from Disney, but it is unfair to expect such high standards to be fulfilled by your spouse. You'll enjoy everything your partner does in the early days of courtship and vice versa, so when you both remain stable, you grow more relaxed in the relationship.

This is where the relationship gets real, and this is where you realize whether your standards are reasonable. The odds of getting them met are high if the aspirations are reasonable.

4. Never lose respect for each other

If you think, passion is enough for a friendship to be sustained, and then think differently. In the end, you will need not only love, but also respect. Even a minor thing like failing to pick up the laundry will end up in an ugly spat if you no longer value your partner. Once the appreciation is gone, the trust will also go out.

So how are you respecting one another? Simply put, express

your partner's gratitude, recognize their sacrifices, listen to their complaints, and hold to your commitments. Small objects like these can have a real influence.

5. Talk to each other, not about each other

Never speak (take) stuff out of the relationship. Your friends may have helped with your struggles before but now things need to change because it is no longer you, but you and your partner. However, if you still need marital advice, try consulting with a psychologist.

Speak to them specifically if you are having a dispute with your partner. In the beginning, it may sound daunting, but you can feel relieved until the weight is off your chest. Such open discussions also lead to building trust and improving the partnership.

6. Do not keep scores

In a game, you establish scores and it is about who wins and who loses. You will win if you add the same to your partnership, but the bond is going to be broken. Typically, couples hold scores to prove their case. It could start with, "Three times in a row I made dinner, and you can't even wash the plate you ate."

If you are facing relentless critique, so try to apologies instead of defending yourself. This will encourage your partner to feel listened to and calm down. This way, you give them a chance to think. But even though they try to demean and belittle you, even after apologizing, then it's time to take a stance, this kind of action is never appropriate and may be a kind of violence. Everyone gets irritated at times; this is a natural human feeling, so it is not acceptable to constantly bring you down.

7. Hate the sin and not the sinner

There are mistakes, things go wrong, and that is life. The problem is under control as long as you both apologize and forgive. Now you have to do that wholeheartedly as you forgive.

Know that recovery can be messy, so all parties have to be very careful and handle it cautiously. Depending on the intensity of the error, it could take days or months. Your companion is injured, or they may be remote actors. In order to get over it, try to learn and motivate them. In addition, after you have made peace with it never hold it against a companion of yours.

8. Fight for what matters

In a friendship, conflicts are inevitable. You cannot stop them, but they can be picked carefully. Ignore the temptation to fight for frivolous problems. When you're about to start a war next time, stop, take a step back and ask yourself if it's worth fighting for, and if the answer is no, trust your instincts and call for a truce.

9. Do not let go of yourself

Before that relationship, you had a life, and you must continue to have one. Just because you are in a relationship with your girlfriend, you don't have to abandon your dreams and live to fulfill them. Build a life outside of your relationship and continue to have one. Get some 'me' time occasionally, head out with your friends or try a hobby.

Understand that in your possession is your pleasure. It doesn't mean that you quit doing positive stuff for each other, just that you are honest about what makes you happy. You will be able to bring love into the relationship until you know it.

10. Do not fight change

A friendship will carry some crucial changes, however awkward they can be. For starters, you might have fun with your friends and go out with them every weekend, but you have to balance your partner and friends while you are in a relationship and your partner will become your focus.

Change will not always be negative; your companion may often carry the change you have been hoping for all your life.

11. Bring out the best in each other

Don't fail to appreciate that your partner is sweet. Write all the positive things of them down, pick one and chat about it with your buddy. If your partner is fantastic at staying cool during a crisis, for example, then ask them how they manage to do it. Your companion would be admired and appreciated in this way.

A working partnership can make both couples feel more relaxed, cure any past emotional trauma, and increase the quality of their lives.

12. Spend time with each other

Couples have to share some quality time with each other, whether it is one year into the relationship or ten years. During the outset of the relationship, they appear to share time with each other but other aspects become more important than the relationship as time progresses.

Don't encourage that to happen to you. Make it a point to speak to your partner and ask them how their day has been no matter how busy you are. If you are not willing to spend time with them, show sincere interest. Be sure you chat on major days, such as birthdays and anniversaries, while you are away from each other. The commitment that you put forward will decide your relationship's success.

13. Divide and conquer

If your partner does not help you, household chores might become frustrating. A partnership can operate smoothly when both parties share the obligations. It does not mean that you plan a military map and demand that it is adhered to by your companion. Discuss and discover common ground. If you are excellent at cooking, for example, and your partner will vacuum, then split the tasks accordingly.

All spouses must know that there are no fixed guidelines for household chores to be completed. If your partner is busy with other tasks, you should volunteer to do their part of the duties, and vice versa.

14. Work as a team

Relationship implies partnership. As long as you are able to tweak them to suit your mate, it is okay to have individual dreams and ambitions. Please speak to your partner before taking any big life decision. Discuss financial matters freely and respect the views of each other. Secrets ruin the spirit of the team and lose faith in the relationship. It's not easy to win it back once trust is lost.

15. Keep the spark alive

Never underestimate physical intimacy's strength. It must not be the one who drives marriage, but making things exciting is important. Touch has the potential to release those hormones, which allow couples to develop an intimate bond. It also aims to improve health and well-being in general.

Book a special trip or a date night where the passion can be rekindled. Be open and chat about your wishes and desires with your partner. In addition, your companion will share the same interests; before you talk, you will never know.

• Conclusion

You would do your hardest to have them by your side if you really love and care for your partner. Getting into a relationship may seem a little easy; it's not a walk in the park to sustain your relationship, however.

You have compromises to make and you have to be able to negotiate. It will help you drive your relationship to greater heights by sticking to these golden relationship guidelines. So stick to them to preserve or move the partnership to the next step.

CHAPTER FIVE

Overcome Anxiety and Jealousies in the Relationship

A prevalent phenomenon is jealousy in marriages. Naturally, when a loved one does not believe you or is wary of you and your climate, this is an uncomfortable feeling. This behaviour will trigger serious issues with relationships. If you are operating on trust, though, then you will conquer envy.

Although we are all jealous from time to time. However, in a relationship, so much and unavoidable envy can be very counterproductive to your union and can save you from enjoyment in life. How can you say if your friendship contains so much jealousy? Clear signs demonstrate unhealthy and pathological envy.

HOW TO RESPOND TO JEALOUSY IN A RELATIONSHIP?

Suspicious behavior is never nice or acceptable for a relationship. The statement of your concern about unjust practice against you is, thus, justified. It is necessary, however, to do so peacefully and decisively, without insulting the partner and without jumping to conclusions.

It is important not to respond impulsively when you find envy in yourself or your partner. Try to decide what caused it, and whether this is a fair source of envy. If you feel unnecessarily liable, then tell your partner about it and reiterate that you do not welcome such conduct.

You should fix the issue easily if the friendship is safe. However when your jealous partner exploits, dominates you, and refuses to speak to you about this issue, if you are stuck in an abusive relationship, then it is crucial to find a way to peacefully end this relationship.

• HOW TO COPE WITH JEALOUSY?

You first need to figure out what triggers it in you in order to conquer envy in a relationship (or your partner). If you have low self-esteem, then you can help conquer envy by focusing on this quality. Try working on it if you have faith challenges triggered by a past relationship. To cope with envy, there are few easy suggestions that everyone should try.

1. Remember That Your Partner Chose You and Not Someone Else

You do have to know that your partner is next to you and he likes and supports you. In addition, if he wanted to be with someone else, then most likely, his friendship with you would be severed. Therefore, he is always with you because he loves someone else and doesn't want to change himself.

2. Work on Your Self-esteem

We also think about ourselves incorrectly and blame our bad emotions on our intimate partners. For starters, if you feel like you are not good enough you are afraid that other people are stronger than you around your loved ones are, and so you start to get angry and jealous.

Most individuals suffer from low self-esteem, and this makes them jealous of the bond. It is also important to be mindful of these emotions in yourself to work to increase your self-esteem, and not to blame anything on your partner. Work to find, and reflect on, good attributes about yourself.

3. The change between a strong and a weak source of jealousy must be known to you.

There's still good proof of healthy jealousy. It may be a text message, for instance, that suggests a person or girl's infidelity. That may be your partner's distant attitude towards you. Jealousy is justified in this situation. However, if you note that a friend of the same sex is talking to your wife and you instantly infer that something is going on with them, then this is an adverse reaction. Without comprehending the case, you should not need to draw hasty assumptions.

4. Try to Be More Gullible

As we don't know how to trust other people, we sometimes start to feel jealous. We may have been misled earlier, but we've lost faith in people. In addition, the fact is that trusting individuals is at higher risk of being robbed. However, to be happy, we must take chances in life.

If you plan to believe your partner and then get disappointed in him, you're going to figure out he's not right for you and you're going to be looking for a new relationship. Alternatively, if you trust him and know that he deserves confidence, then the friendship will grow much more, and all of you will become happier people. However, if you place limitations on yourself or your partner, you will not do anything and will constantly show mistrust.

• Overcome Anxiety

Relationships are emotionally intense, partially because of the closeness that you share with another person. This familiarity makes you insecure, unfortunately, which can lead to nervousness and insecurity, particularly if you are susceptible to both. Stress is a fear of what might happen, while insecurity is about doubting yourself and not having confidence. Uncertainty causes fear, too. There are ways to cope with your relationship issues and insecurities, which will cultivate a bond with your partner that is mentally safe, happy, and comfortable.

- **DEALING WITH ANXIETY ABOUT YOUR RELATIONSHIP**

1. Recognize That You Feel Fear

Differentiating healthy nervousness and anxiety from harmful and excessive stress is complicated. You may suffer from anxiety about your relationship or even an anxiety disorder if you find that your problem is affecting your life or your relationship. Speak to a psychiatrist if you believe this might be the problem, and make positive mental improvements. We've had the following of the symptoms of anxiety:

- Worrying excessively
- Sleep disturbances
- Chronic indigestion
- Depression Sweating

2. Find out the Cause of Your Concern

Typically, uncertainty about a relationship is a result of an inherent insecurity. This would be beneficial in taking care of your emotions and reducing your fear once, you recognise these insecurities. You can find that you are experiencing tension, but without understanding the cause. Think on what makes you nervous and how you can concentrate on your own confusion. Doctors assume that even individuals who are still vulnerable to anxiety, life's stressful events will lead to anxiety disorders. We will inherit traits of anxiety as well.

Related to some medical disorders, such as thyroid issues, diabetes, heart disease, irritable bowel syndrome, substance addiction, respiratory problems, and chronic pain symptoms, anxiety can occur. Speak to a psychiatrist to rule out underlying health conditions if you believe you suffer from anxiety. In addition, request a therapist's assistance to overcome the pain that could be the source of the anxiety in your life.

3. You Can Go to Couples Therapy

This does not mean your friendship is weak or broken if you request treatment as a partner. That also means you and your partner will take advantage by turning to a qualified specialist to help them overcome issues of connectivity, vulnerability, and privacy. This may also mean that if they undergo pair counselling, they both want the relationship to be good and that the couple agrees that they could benefit from mutual assistance.

Likely, a couple's psychiatrist will not serve you and your wife separately, as this might cause a conflict of interest. As a protective measure, several partners request counselling, particularly though both of them are not nervous about the relationship.

4. Evaluate Your Relationship

To decide if it adds to your insecurities and anxieties, you can objectively analyze your friendship. You might find that you are in a relationship that is dysfunctional or violent and that your stress is triggered by this flaw. You can note, on the other hand, that you are in a very safe relationship and that you must concentrate on yourself. When you see that you are in an unhappy relationship, decide what the next step is going to be whether the relationship is going to be counselling or over.

If you were in an abusive relationship, your friends and relatives would be superb markers who will show it to you. They tell you that you have different talents, or make dumb reasons for not meeting you and your partner. They might tell you right away that they don't like your wife, or they might always chat of a time when you were single and happy. To bear in mind, these are critical remarks.

• DEAL WITH INSECURITIES ABOUT YOUR RELATIONSHIP

1. Know Your Inner Critic

Getting an inner critic is healthy; but if it speaks too much or is too loud, you can begin to feel uncomfortable. Listen, critically, to the inner critic. Find out what makes you self-doubt. The progression in insecurity will interrupt or slow down so that it does not become anxiety when you separate critical thoughts and focus on your dreams, not the emotions associated with them. Few examples of critical thought are here:

- Either way, you will be hurt.
- That person is too right for you.
- When you know your true self, you will dislike it.
- You will get bored with time. You are not attractive enough.

2. Put Your Inner Critic in His Place

Create a list of meticulous ideas you have that are recurring. In addition, when you feel a little relaxed, review the list. In contrast to concepts that sound impractical, focus on what sounds justified or practical. Often, think of the generalizations that you have made and whether or not you feel they are valid. Check off something that sounds unrealistic or irrational on your list and start coping healthily and productively with these picky ideas.

3. Analyze Your Past

Through previous encounters, insecurities also emerge. Focus on events from the life that in the current may have led to your uncertainties. Such interactions do not have to rely solely on marriages; at your school, with your friends, in love, and with family, consider relationships and talents. Can you think about something that has arisen in the moment that could lead to your insecurities or anxieties?

Someone may have made a joke about your intellect or your looks. A friend may have arranged for you and then left you standing, hurting you and making you feel worthless. Perhaps a parent or teacher for not having excelled at anything scolded you.

4. Stop Comparing Yourself

Much as insecurities derive from previous interactions, through those that we model and our past relationships, we learn how to be in relationships. This would be damaging if you equate your current relation to all of your past links, which will only make you doubt yourself. Your current partner is special, and you are different from what you have been during all of your past partnerships. Similarly, do not slip into the pit of likening yourself to the ex-partners of your new girlfriend. For whatever excuse, your partner is with you and not with them, and there is no reason to equate yourself to anyone your partner is no longer with.

COMMUNICATE WITH YOUR PARTNER

1. Don't Expect Your Lover to Read Your Attention

You can read your account as much as you can but you can't ask your partner to know what you think and feel. You may believe the interaction or circumstance is reasonably obvious, and since your partner does not respond the way you thought it should, you may feel more uncomfortable or nervous.

You may think, on the other hand, that you made it clear that you hate the action, but your partner does not seem to have understood how you feel. Don't ask me to see things like you or to know what you are feeling and thinking.

2. Talk to Your Partner

Just as if your lover cannot read your attention, if you do not say them, they can never know what you feel. When you do not feel nervous, talk to your partner about your thoughts and desires. It is important that you express these items and that you encourage them to respond to you. Before starting the chat, be simple, succinct, and plan what you want to talk about.

- Write A List If Necessary

Be specific about the insecurities and anxieties. Don't generalize and, where you can, take note of the source of the issues. Concentrate on the actions, the reactions, and the solution. Do not attribute finger signals or fault. I know I must be more polite, and in a cautious moment, I need you to respond to my texts, so I will not start worrying.

3. Keep Talking

On the part of both parties, stable partnerships take continuous commitment, and this means holding the communication lines open. Do not believe that with a discussion about your thoughts with your girlfriend, you can fix everything. Even by manipulating your thoughts and completely releasing them in an interview, do not overwhelm your spouse. Instead, in their friendship, bring them into the habit of having brief, regular talks.

An outstanding solution is to set aside 15 minutes a day to speak to your partner. Ask each other questions that are open-ended and listen carefully to their responses. These could be some of your questions: "What would you like to try but are you too scared?" "Tell me about your dream vacation," "Tell me in detail about an event that you think has changed you a lot, be it good or bad."

4. Touch Each Other

Kisses, smiles, and various forms of physical affection can reinforce the relational bond you have with your partner. Bear in mind that touch is an important part of a relationship, even though you feel nervous or irritated, and it is soothing for both you and your partner. If at a given moment, one of you does not need to be affected, talk about your emotions, and value the other's space.

For different levels of intimacy, there are various kinds of physical contact. You'll like an intimate or romantic contact with your partner, which involves embracing, kissing, touching the face, and caressing.

If it is more relaxed, put your arm around your companion or put him around you.

- Put your arm around your partner or put his around you if that is more comfortable.
- Hug your partner and hold the hug for a longer time than usual.
- Concentrate on the closeness that you both share.
- Hold hands.
- Kiss each other.
- Pick up the hair from your face.

Dealing with anxieties or insecurities recurring

1. Talk to a Doctor

If you find that you experience tension or insecurity about your relationship, do not categorize yourself as a jealous or lousy person for relationships. Don't really downplay your emotions. Your fear of your relationship may be unfounded, you may know, but you may not know how to avoid it. You might suffer from a genuine anxiety condition that can be treated by a doctor. Chat about your fear to a psychiatrist or counselor, so you can decide whether you need to get care.

2. Be yourself

Your freedom should still be maintained and your sense of identity secured. Your life is complemented by that of your mate, and it must be a two-person alliance. If you drop into your association, you can be too focused on validations from your mate, contributing to increased fear and vulnerability.

There is a contrast between the partner reaching a common understanding and giving up your sense of belonging. To give and receive though giving is just giving is a mutual understanding.

Do not look at your partner for protection. When you feel nervous or worried about your relationship, the only thing you want is that your husband tells you that all is good and he is satisfied with you. Unfortunately, this makes your emotions rely on your partner's validation and because she has criminal accountability for your feelings. Don't forget that your thoughts are yours and don't depend on anybody, your wife included.

3. Keep Busy

Information suggests that this will help to reduce your feelings of fear and uncertainty whether you keep yourself busy emotionally or physically. The definition is that doing emotional or physical exercise allows you to focus mental resources on something other than the relationship's insecurities and fears. You can feel it as a diversion at first; however, it can become a fun habit and a way to get off steam if you continue doing the operation.

- You can join a gym and commit to following an exercise schedule.
- Sign up to volunteer frequently, like on Saturdays at your local animal shelter.
- Practice gardening or other outdoor activities.
- Learn a language.
- Participate in a reading club.

4. Give up a Little Control

To ensure that everything happens, as it should and that you can fulfill your desires, you can find that you have to regulate your relationship. You certainly don't know, on the other hand, that you are manipulating your partner to ease your insecurities. One thing is that you are not going to encourage your partner to share in the relationship fairly. The other concern is that in your relationship, you would be too focused on how something happens. Your fear is likely to intensify if anything arises outside of your influence.

You shouldn't base your emotions on the level of power you have over your relationship in order to preserve your identity.

Initially, having your partnership behave as a relationship may be awkward, but this will encourage your partner to affirm your emotions and relieve your insecurities, as it will act out of its own free will.

5. Give Yourself Support

It is easy to disown yourself, particularly if you find that any of your emotions might be unreasonable, because you feel uncomfortable or nervous about your relationship. Offer yourself help, rather than belittle yourself for exploring vulnerability. Imagine the way of talking to a mate who looks like you.

This might sound odd to you at first if you speak to yourself positively, but with experience, it will get simpler and seem more normal. Recognize your thoughts, and then make a deliberate attempt to reformulate your mindset so that help can be given.

Imagine, for instance, that your partner is going to attend a work event, and since spouses or couples are not invited, you feel awkward. You tell your wife your way of thinking, and she gets mad. Say something like, "I'm happy that I expressed my feelings and did it calmly." instead of feeling guilty about bothering her.

In addition, if he or she told you that they would be studying, you might still feel worried that your companion is not answering the call. You'll realize why you may overreact, but you'll still feel nervous. "I am proud of myself for acknowledging that my reaction is inadequate and for understanding that my partner needs time to study, and that does not take her away from our relationship. "I am proud of myself for acknowledging that my response is incomplete and for knowing that my partner needs time to research, and that does not take her away from our relationship.

- Tips to deal with your anxiety.

  - Volunteering
  - Writing
  - Painting
  - Video games
  - Exercise, and
  - Friends are good examples.

- **MANAGE STRESS AND BUILD A SOLID RELATIONSHIP**

• Stress in The relationship

Stress creates complications in the relationship and develops a vicious spiral of toxic feelings that hinder coordination, causing disagreements that damage each of them's personal lives.

Stress is a natural response, experienced and endured by all human beings. It is generally a matter of interest in couple of relationships because of the ramifications that can occur when its management is uncertain and the different forms of dealing with it. Therefore, I want to share with you today how to handle your relationship tension.

The biggest downside is recognizing that tension is a sign of a red flag, that is, that things are not right, and the fact that it is present. Therefore, the inference is drawn that the relationship is not on the right track or on the other hand, stop it at all costs or are so engaged in worrying about its existence that you fail to look at ways to deal with it.

Any participant of the partnership, or the relationship itself would not benefit from any of those two acts. The appearance of tension in a few relationships is not representative of issues, which is why it is important to redefine what stress is and what suggests its presence in many relationships.

• Stress in a Relationship Can Occur for Various Reasons

The family and individual burden that each individual may have for jobs, home management, finances, personal or technical fulfillment. It will lead to disagreements, estrangement, to make one of the members realize that the other does not respect him and is not for him or her. Mishandling him on your own.

Because of conflict resolution, decision-making, disputes, boundaries, bargaining, little or no connection, the tension of the relationship. Let's Grasp Tension (That is, the stress caused by their members not being able to reach agreements on issues vital to them, one making decisions alone or alone and the other not being assertive in expressing disagreement if applicable.)

• Let's Know Stress

Stress is a normal reaction of the human body (physiological and psychological), which naturally reacts to conditions that are difficult for the individual undergoing them. All these factors cause the couple to evolve, much as the human being is in continual transition, and development, as well as the relationship of the couple, is in perpetual growth, maturation phase, new perceptions and experiences, and so a certain amount of tension is required for the body to react to changes and challenges.

In stressful circumstances that need a new approach, tension occurs in many relationships. Learn to overcome these disputes so that you can boost your quality of life by having a closer relationship with your partner. Living together often creates tension and disagreements that can be necessary for the relationship to be handled and above all, can be overcome effectively.

If you don't face them, these disputes expand, and on the contrary, you neglect them for fear they are going to get bigger. Problems must immediately be understood and acknowledged such that both may find an answer to them.

Both have to examine and evaluate what is happening and be mindful of the ideals and desires they have of each other, including the differences that may arise, to exist in peace and develop emotionally in the relationship. The tension in the relationship is induced by trouble with kids, of the two or both addictions, by either financial problems or intimacy issues, envy or infidelity of one of the two.

• He Loves Me; He Doesn't Love Me

In a relationship, there are problems that trigger tension, such as not being positive whether your partner likes you. Many inexperienced partners think, "If my partner loves me, I will be pleased with what I ask." That's a false idea that can harm the relationship or trigger problems that are more serious.

Not feeling liked several times at the level of couples is not usually a reality. The customs, upbringing, and traditions of your partner will affect your relationship with your partner and make you feel unloved, though they are not.

These erroneous views, which cause relationship issues, are also not synonymous with a lack of affection. They may be triggered by various personality traits, myths and explanations are false or attributable to personal issues, etc. Yet many think and see this as a loss of affection, and depression is caused by that.

• Opinions of Third Parties

A couple's partnership is a relationship between two, and since there are unique difficulties that are very typical of them, no one can meddle with opinions.

There are facets of the relationship that can not be discussed with relatives or close friends and even though they have the right intentions to help you fix issues, others' perspectives will trigger unintended tension.

• Intimacy Is Two

Intimacy refers to a bond that two individuals share based on physical and emotional encouragement, trust, and independence, culminating in a stable connection. In the intimacy context, if you do not communicate with your mate, it could cause pain and anguish: intimacy rises and decreases in conjunction with the tension experienced by both of you.

When one of you is depressed, the other should know that for a moment his tension calms down, it is better to leave him alone.

• Decisions

When they have to make a decision, another aspect that creates tension in a marriage, because they must obviously choose to make it because the decision affects the house, children and other family members will be influenced by the decision for better or worse.

One of the two attempts to exert power over the other several times in this decision-making to persuade him, and that brings about the discussions and the altercations for discrepancies in the points of view of both.

• The Finances

Another challenge causing tension in the relationship is finances, which is one of the most critical stressors, based on research carried out by researchers, since one of the two wants to invest more than the other is, while the partner likes to plan.

This causes the pair to experience depression if the income is too poor so they do not cover the bills on time, and particularly if they have multiple credit cards, it can be much more difficult to face the expenses of the family.

The best thing to do to prevent tension at the level of partners is outstanding contact to be able to cope successfully with stress-causing issues. There is no more important tension than being frustrated over overheated conversations with your partner.

When you are both relaxed and able to address the challenges that you have to tackle together, it is easier to discuss things.

- **How to Build a Strong Relationship?**

Let us imagine that you wanted a house to be built. In the middle of an open area, you are standing and thinking about how to do it. You have options: you can study building literature, you can see how others build, you can ask for help from experienced builders, or you can try to make it yourself as it goes.

In addition, because it is easier and quicker, you choose the last option. You look around in some places, stones lie, trees are growing somewhere, and sand and other improvised materials lie. You take them and start building." Make your calculations known only to you according to some scheme, put a pebble on a pebble and rejoice that everything turns out so fast. Then when the house grows, surprises start to take place: the sand is crumbling, the stones are rupturing, and the bars are not converging.

In addition, you start getting nervous and angry. While continuing to build further, you are desperate to patch holes. It appears to you as the best is being sought. However, in the end, you wake up one day and you see your whole house collapsing. In addition, you accuse building materials furiously of their inappropriateness. Now with a lot of time and effort spent in vain, you are sitting in the middle of an open area without a house, without the desire to start over. Then you intend to build a new home instead.

In the same way, and, suddenly, lucky this time. In addition, that continues.

• And What about the Relationship?

Let's think that the most complex of living systems is man. He has a body, a conscience, thoughts, impulses, memories, perceptions, wounds, and so on. Both these "building materials" are much darker than sand, bricks, and timber and are more nuanced. That is unmatched. Do you believe that just like that you would build harmonious relationships? Without expertise, without other people's wisdom and the assistance of the wise? You can construct it somehow, of course, but then you can somehow feel yourself with this entity. In addition, anything will crumble in a day. Therefore, we're going to criticize him and the male gender as a whole for being rascals. No we just don't know who we're developing relationships with and how.

Nobody taught us this. In college, we were required to study well, take tests, and earn money. Perhaps most notably, no one told us that these are intimate relationships. As if, we were not human beings, but insensitive vehicles.

However, yes, we are humans. In addition, we need a healthy friendship with ourselves and with others for satisfaction.

Therefore, let's understand.

1. Plan

No wonder the "build." link looks like building a home. Second, in your head, you and your chosen one must build a strategy. The other person and you need to consider what they expect from marriages, from each other and from life. How much and what you would like to get, how much and what you are willing to give. Example: do you want to live in a village in a small house? Alternatively, in a city center apartment? Alternatively, not finding a home and working my entire life? We require different partners for various purposes. In the first scenario, it is fitting you to be a peasant, in the second - a famous businessperson, in the third - and an everlasting traveller. You would feel much more relaxed if you initially understand that you have common beliefs and plans for life. Your beloved, after all is a life-long friend, and you ought to make sure you're going one direction. Think for yourself why give up on an explosion of passion if you want to survive in the city and milk your cows? What's going to bring you? Disappointment and suffering, it feels.

2. The Foundation

In addition, the most thrilling part starts - finding out yourself - when you have already noticed that you are on the road and you have feelings for this person. Are you sure of why families are crumbling? All feels we need to make that move. Changing yourself is the secret to a happier relationship. It is complicated, it is painful, it takes time and commitment, but if you want to have a substantial home, it is important. What you ask the other one is fleeting; for life, what you find and correct about yourself. If all couples focus on themselves frankly and support each other genuinely, so they discover a gift - relationship. Your cornerstone is selfless friendship.

3. Roof

In life, many interesting things happen. Woe and pleasure, riches and hunger, health and disease. Life will always be anything to satisfy you before the end comes. Do you know why all of it is happening? It is to test the strength of our emotions and ourselves. For a huge, substantial house full of love and warmth, people who pass all tests with integrity and together obtain a reward; thus, fidelity is your home's roof. The more durable it is the more peaceful your life will be. Fidelity is not when we do not abandon an individual, whether we do not have somewhere else to go, we do not want to do things, or we have not found anyone else. Fidelity is when you can do all of the above in a challenging situation, but you do not really have a feeling like this because together.

4. Walls

What is going to happen within your home's walls is your

decision. There you can dance, cook, raise kids, meditate - it does not matter. If you have a dream, a base, and a roof, then it will bring you pleasure, whatever you do.

The primary issue, after all, is not what," but how."

Accordingly:

- Recognize your desires, life goals and build a plan
- Pray, meditate, associate with saints, and cleanse your foundation
- Learn to help people around, even if the problem seems insoluble. Without a roof now impossible.

If you have these three elements, you will have everything.

• What Is the Difference Between Fear and Anxiety: Differentiation of Concepts?

Most contemporaries agree that the same words, which are the same designation of a certain state of a person, are terror and anxiety. However, there are many basic variations between the emotion of fear and feelings of anxiety, it should be remembered. Fear is a particular natural response that arises in reaction to the action of a specific stimulus. A warning is a situation that happens without a clear signal being present. Now of the onset of an extreme situation, anxiety arises in a person automatically. Long before the root of the danger, fear overcomes the subject. Fear reflects on a particular risk source that exists and is knowledgeable of a person; the fear of being bitten by a snake, for instance, comes from the presence of a reptile. In expectation of a collision with a source of risk, fear appears; an individual cannot clarify the presence of this sensation. In most cases, anxiety is associated with the suppression of mental processes and activation of the nervous system's parasympathetic parts. This emotion paralyzes or causes him to take off, "rivets" a person in place. In conjunction with unnecessary excitement of the sympathetic portions of the nervous system, fear is twisted.

This emotion does not cause the subject to function in the normal way of life and totally covers a person's mind. Fear is focused on current human experience, on traumatic incidents that have happened in the past. Anxiety is often based on the future; it is a particular sense of dread of an impending stressful encounter.

• Why Anxiety Arises: Causes of Obsessive Feeling

Anxiety does not have sufficient triggers, unlike normal emotion - anxiety, which happens when there is a specific source of threat and is the body's reaction to the effects of intense external stimuli. The explanation why he had a sense of fear can not be identified and clarified by a person. The person predicts the onset of certain problems, in the absence of signs of the presence of actual risk, although he does not have the solution and expertise to solve possible problems. A long-lasting feeling of undefined, incomprehensible obsessive terror is the sense of anxiety.

In the moment, this feeling does not have any real motives and is still geared towards the future. The cause of fear is still focused on true personal experience or is based on previous examples linked to adverse incidents around us in the world. An entity independently looks for any signs of negativity in his life past or knowledge that remains in his memories and passes the information obtained to the future.

Through cases, we demonstrate. The topic, having found a dog, remembers that when a flock of stray animals bit him, there was a situation in that dog's life. An individual has a sense of fear because he is certain that a disaster will recur.

In addition, anxiety does not only overpower a person due to the occurrence of any tragic events in his personal history.

Stress is always focused on the object that induced strangers to have drama.

An individual declines to use air travel, for example, having read enough news of air accidents, so she is convinced that she will inevitably become a victim of an airplane accident.

Such causes, which are not at all related to incidents in the personal life of an individual, can frequently contribute to the emergence of absurd obsessive fear, which has a huge effect on actions and worldview. A rational and uncontrollable anxiety prohibits a basic active lifestyle from being led by the client and is the leading cause of neurosis.

For example, in a distant world, an entity who has read details regarding the outbreak starts to take needless precautions: declines to use certain goods, inappropriately using disinfectants, ceases to be in public areas.

The unique personality constitution of the organism is one of the leading causes of obsessive anxiety. There is a high probability that paranoid, impressionable, suspicious individuals may experience abnormal feelings of anxiety. The appearance of this disorder is often predisposed to people who have a high level of stress. Such subjects respond very violently to the effects of any stimulus, even of insignificant strength.

The presence of hypertrophied shame in individual and groundless ideas about his guilt are another reason for the occurrence of anxiety. The development of obsessive states is predisposed to an individual who is convinced that it is he who is the source of all problems and problems.

In subjects who are ashamed of some of their actions or are shy of their personality, pathological anxiety also often occurs. A common reason for the appearance of abnormal obsessive states is the presence of an inferiority complex, a denial of their identity, a lack of understanding of personal traits.

The persistence of the subject's unhealthy fear of loss is also the source of the production of anxiety. Such disruptive individuals are vulnerable to any criticism addressed to them, and they are afraid to hear information about the poor quality of their activities. They are very sensitive to any words sent in their direction, and want to get their value confirmed at all times.

CONCLUSION

What is Relationship Anxiety? Where does it originate from and how to get over it are the fundamental and overwhelming questions that are being addressed by all those engaged in various kinds of troubled relationships? Anxiety in relationships starts when you begin to feel that your partner is no longer attracted to you. How do you justify feeling this way? She doesn't get as excited about your coming home from work as she used to. You get nervous and start to wonder what is wrong with yourself or your partner, and why things might not be the same as they were at the beginning of your relationship. Your anxiety increases as you think more and more about this and it turns into what psychiatrists describe and label as relationship anxiety.

You get perplexed and annoyed when your partner does not respond to your tests quickly or when you get worried about her feelings for you in your absence. You start thinking that when you are not around, your partner does not miss you anymore. She does not enjoy your jokes and does not laugh at them. You start to take a humble view of yourself, believing that your looks have been lost.

There is this feeling that because there is something wrong with you and the way you behave, your partner does not enjoy your business. Your partner needs someone better, someone who is smarter, financially strong, and good at keeping her amused most of the time, you begin to presume. All of this makes you think that you have lost interest in your partner, and your relationship is headed to failure.

Most of you could have been at one end of the above-mentioned scenario or the other. Either you could have been a worrier, or you could have been someone related to the worrier. There is also a great probability of both situations being experienced by you. It is first-hand knowledge that the feeling of insecurity is the mother of all adverse thoughts, and our closest relationships are extremely bad. Anxiety in relationships can travel from one partner to another. However because it came from you and no one else, it is only you who can cure it!

It is not surprising that individuals with low self-esteem show further insecurity in relationships. Consequently, it prevents such people from enjoying the benefits of a loving connection. It is simply because individuals with low self-esteem want their partners to have a better assessment of them. In addition, being victims of cynicism, they find it difficult and difficult to recognize and accept their partner's assertions. Consequently, they may push the partner away because of developed insecurities. This is an internal and perpetual struggle that has nothing to do with circumstances, you must remember. In dealing with your insecurities, it is therefore crucial that you not distort or drag your loved one into them. By uncovering the real cause of your insecurity and confronting the inside one that threatens your relationship, this can be achieved.

Old affections from your past are shaping your relationships. All of you have established relationship mindsets that have been developed with powerful caretakers in your attachments.

Your previous experiences in life can influence your adult relationships and shape them. In the choice of your partners, attachment style plays an important role. A secure attachment style typically helps you display more confidence and self-control. On the contrary, you are very likely to be susceptible to the feeling of insecurity towards your partner if you have an anxious attachment style.

Awareness and knowledge of your attachment style is extremely beneficial as it promotes the selection of the best partner and thus creates healthier relationships.

Your insecurities may arise from your inner voice as well. For instance, if you lived with parents who hated themselves or criticized your behavior, you begin to internalize this style of attachment. It stays with you until, for your greater benefit, you try to address it positively. This inner voice, moreover, has a direct negative effect on your relationships. By convincing you about the negative changes in your partner's behavior towards you, it can fuel doubts about your girlfriend's interest in you. Your mind is occupied by anxious thoughts that your partner is going to reject you.

You are jolted by relationships. They hit the basic feelings you have about yourself hard. You are pulled out of your comfort zones by relationships. If you were abandoned in, infancy by your parents, your romantic partner's identical attitude and approach would not have the same impact on your mental status. It can throw you back into the complex state of some frightened child who desperately needs the support of parents for survival.

So what is salvation from a precarious scenario like that? You need to have the courage and determination to challenge this skepticism towards yourselves as a first resort. You should do all that you can to defy your inner voice's commands. You need your independence to hold on. It is very important to maintain a sense of yourself that is different from your partner. Your identity must not be renounced. You both need to stick to the unique characteristics that in the earlier phase of the relationship brought you together.

You must not allow your insecurity to galvanize you with destructive behavior. Remember that your relationship can be harmful to feelings of irrational display or jealousy of possessive conduct. Respect your partner's privacy and don't try to read messages about your partner. Through your frequent calls, you must not annoy them. Do not get flared up by their gratifying remarks about a beautiful person. Regardless of how hurtful they are to you, you must avoid these acts. You will feel more powerful and more confident by avoiding these acts. When your partner reciprocates identically, you will both have a greater sense of mutual trustworthiness.

Since we can change our part of the scenario, it's also worth talking about whether there are any actions that we do that drive our mate away. D If we do things that we appreciate and then don't feel like we deserve what we need, we should make a deliberate effort to talk about it or change the scenario with our companion, and we have never had to feel betrayed or encourage ourselves to act in ways that we don't respect.

You must not seek the reassurance of your partner. You will stop re-evaluating and re-assessing the behavior of your partner. You have to embrace your partner's uniqueness and individuality. You need negative tendencies and attitudes to be overcome. You should be open enough to accept your partner's love and affection. You must not be satisfied with someone in a relationship who is not sincere, but who needs to find someone who loves you. For a happy, peaceful and worry-free life, a relationship that is based on reciprocity in terms of love, affection, kindness, trust, allegiance, maturity, and devoid of insecurities, anxiety, negative thoughts, and irrational behavior will be conducive.

Book 2

RELATIONSHIP COMMUNICATION FOR COUPLES

The Ultimate Guide to Learn How to Improve Your Couple Communication and Discover the 25 Skills to Grow a Deeper Connection

INTRODUCTION

Good communication is an important aspect of all communications and is a required part of a good relationship. Partnerships have difficulties, but a constructive style of communication would make the settlement of conflicts easier and create a stronger and healthier partnership. We often learn how important dialogue is but not what it is and how to use productive interaction in our relationships.

By essence, correspondence is the act of transmitting information from one location to the other. Communication in relationships allows you to explain what you believe and what your expectations are with someone else. The act of communicating not only makes you satisfy your needs, it also encourages you to truly speak in your relationship.

The very essence of the relationship can be harmed by the consequences of bad contact. The symptoms of relationship breakdown include the impression of the other person that they are not understood, constantly arguing, assuming that nothing is being addressed on the issue at hand, and actively behaving. Bad communication can cause difficulties with self-esteem and self-confidence.

Transparency, honesty, accessibility, and respect for each

other are the foundation of strong relations. The path to developing more productive, caring and supportive relationships is focused on acquiring good communication skills, perhaps the most important component of successful interpersonal interaction. In terms of expressing an understanding of the other person's experience, empathic engagement is key.

Another component of the effectiveness of relationships is the ability to stay dependent on the other person, the moment and the feelings. Relationships are founded on consensus and finding mutually agreeable solutions, taking care of yourself and others, pretending to be a tyrant in a relationship just doesn't work.

Two forms of speech exist: verbal and nonverbal. Each one is just as important as the other is. This will work together to convey information. If people may not use their language to say what they think or feel, they will instead act out. All discussions also help well to illustrate a critical message; this is only the case, though if they encourage open communication with their spouse.

• How communication is critical in one's relationship:

Many that do not engage with others do not transmit a part of themselves. They stick to their feelings and perceptions with many unique motivations. People refuse to connect because they risk disappointment because of relationship troubles, because they are afraid that they will do something or say something that will offend their partner. While the above feeling is noteworthy, not asking your partner what you need stops the partnership from adapting and changing. If you would like it to be long-lived as well as satisfying, development is key in a relationship.

• Prevent confusion

Another important cause for interaction is that there is often misunderstanding between people. Each partner can regard various situations that can create anger and other feelings of hurt. Partners may get angry at each other without contact, without ever understanding why or how it began. Effective communication may give rise to planned behaviour and concern for the emotions of each other.

• Laying down expectations

If a couple mentions clearly, what their expectations are it is impossible for them to disregard those norms. No one will say, "How was I meant to know that you don't like it when I contact other women on the internet?" When the other person made it very clear that they wanted you not to email other women online. There is no question about what is acceptable and as a result, how each group feels as expectations are established and adopted.

• Understand the other

Partners who do not communicate may fall into an unpleasant habit of only being with each other and never knowing each other well. A relationship does not get very deep until the connection is straightforward and normal.

Another explanation a couple cannot communicate is because both agree that if they address the problem, it will only make things worse. Perhaps this kind of couple loves each other but without hurting the relationship, they do not understand how to handle difficult subjects. Couples begin weakening their connection when worrying about things or even logical thoughts and feelings. Quite definitely, your relationship with your wife formed out of sharing stuff you both wanted to talk about. When you stop talking, you will break the connection.

CHAPTER ONE

Why Communication Is Important

Perhaps the most essential of all fundamental skills is getting the option to connect effectively. That thing punishes us for handing on data to others and for doing what is alleged to us. You only have to watch a boy enthusiastically attend to his mother and attempt to rehash the sounds she makes to see how energetic the inclination to convey is. Communication is the sit-in of moving data, at its minimum bleak, first with one ad, then into the next. Its ability is expressive (using voice), unruffled (using written or internet media, such as books, journals, blogs or emails), external (uncontrolled icons, guides, systems or charts) or non-verbally (utilizing non-verbal communication, motions and the tone and pitch of voice). By and by, it is always a combination of a couple of these. It may take a lifetime to ace for partnership skills; on the unlikely risk that indeed someone would ever profess to have aced them. There are, however, several steps that you can do politically to restore your relationship skills and guarantee that you can adequately convey and acquire knowledge.

It is the shared substance data to incorporate. The information is exchanged between people. Correspondence further reveals knowledge on how individuals relate and how relations between individuals are communicated through thought, talking, tuning in, deciphering, learning, and reacting.

Almost all, including verbally articulated sentences, sounds, body stance, email, and even quietness, is a means of correspondence. Indeed, even not speaking is a way of imparting, as it can also retain meaning, respect, and pass on knowledge in itself.

For example, when her folks are arguing, a high school little girl falls silent and throws her eyes down onto the floor. For e.g., this demonstration of silence will pass on some important knowledge about social intricacies and how the little girl feels, "If it's not too much trouble, keep me separate from this. It alarms me when you battle and I want to close down."

The massive audience never found out how to express it. Without this skill, a participant in a personal relationship is impaired. Accomplices can not gain closeness without providing the option to connect and tuning in to another. You and your accomplice will have the chance to create and protect the deferential bond between two people who love each other by building up your relationship skills.

The most important concern in imparting is undoubtedly that most partners have a false judgment about what the motive behind communication is. Most of the technique converses as a conversation with an accomplice in which both offers a skewed rendition of the reality of what occurs between the two accomplices.

The drawback in this approach is the mixed-up presumption that any accomplice will enter the argument with a precise vision of the real world. It's outside the realm of imagination because neither one has the critical knowledge to find out what the reality is that is, what's going on between them.

Figuring out what the fact is is one explanation for communication. As they express and examine the whole of their discernments, emotions, opinions and contemplations and go to an exact interpretation of what is going on the letter involves the coordinated work of two people.

Law to obey before entering into a dialogue with your accomplice: incapacitate singularly. That is, surrender ought to be right! You don't stroll into a fight you ought to win. It is not always the case for you to negotiate or abdicate.

It's not always the case that you can't get mad, upset or inspired. In all of your contemplations and feelings, you reserve a right. Only remember that there might be a comment from your accomplice that merits tuning in and contemplating. This dialog is not where you can prove that you are right; it is anything but a fight you should win.

• Why Is It Important

Correspondence is the demonstration of transferring knowledge from one location, individual or set to another. Each correspondence involves one sender, a message and a receiver (in any case). This can sound basic, but communication is an exceptionally mind-boggling subject.

The delivery of the message from the source to the beneficiary may be affected by an enormous scope of items. This include our mental state, the social environment, the medium used to interact, and our country. The difficulty is the reason why bosses everywhere deem suitable relational skills so attractive: accurate, convincing and unambiguous communications is rather challenging.

The sender, normally in a combination of words and non-verbal correspondence, encodes the message. It is communicated here and there (in conversation or composting, for example), and it is 'disentangled' by the beneficiary. There may be more than one receiver, and the unpredictability of communication ensures that a marginally specific message will be read by anyone. In the collection of words as well as non-verbal communication, two people can add different items. Moreover, it is possible that none of them would have the same extraordinary expertise as the sender.

The jobs of the sender and the receiver in intimate and personal communications is not unmistakable. The two places will go back and two people will learn of advances. The two players communicate to each other, regardless of whether, for example, by the eye-to-eye connection (or absence of and general non-verbal contact, in incredibly inconspicuous ways. Be it as it can, the sender and beneficiary are increasingly unmistakable in composed correspondence.

The different classifications of communications include:

They were oral or Visual Contact, which involves close and personal communication, internet, radio or television, and other newspapers.

• Non-Verbal Communication:

Covering non-verbal contact, gestures, where we pose, how we dress or behave, and even our scent. There are different inconspicuous ways in which we interact with others (maybe even unexpectedly). The medium of talking, for example, may provide temperament or excited state with bits of details, while hand signals or gestures can contribute to an orally communicated message.

• Written Communication:

That involves emails, texts, books, journals, the Web, and other mass media, online life. Up to this point, when it came to imparting the composed word, an abstemiously modest number of journalists and distributors were groundbreaking. Today, we can all create and allocate our views on the internet, which has sparked a blast of opportunities for information and correspondence.

• HOW BETTER COMMUNICATION LEADS TO A HEALTHIER MARRIAGE.

In any friendship, outstanding contact is the primary pillar. Communication is the vehicle by which all other essential elements of a partnership are constructed. If you love someone, but you do not use your language or acts to connect with him or her, then you are wrong. It is important that you let them know when you trust someone, respect someone or appreciate someone and the best way to do that is through contact. The foundation of a kind, stable and safe marriage or partnership is truthful contact. Communication achieved in the correct approach continues to be a long loving relationship or a short loving relationship the only doorway to either relationship weather.

When a relationship is full of passion, loyalty, integrity and every other outstanding attribute, since these attributes do not stand by themselves, it also needs contact. Only by the expression of these characteristics that can only be accomplished by communication can a marriage worth envying be created. The precise moment where your marriage will go from good to high is where you will connect with your partner and let them know how much they matter to you. Communication is more than simply communicating or listening to each other, though. It is possible to identify communication as verbal communication or nonverbal

154

communication.

• Verbal communication

Words have meaning, and the words spoken have life. They can be created or broken by the words you say your mate. When they hear kind words like you are cherished, and you look amazing, everybody appreciates the words of spoken contact that help you communicate how you feel to your partner. When you love someone with all you might, and you may not take the time to express it enough the odds are that the other person will never realize how much they are cherished. In addition, if you love your partner, letting them know that they are valued is important. Asking your partner how you see them and your feelings on them lets them get a sense of just how you feel about them.

You are asking about something you want in the same way; you should be able to talk about what you don't like, just in a respectful, caring manner. There is entirely inseparable contact and marital satisfaction. If your partner does something that irritates you, then you don't say if they're going to continue to do so unknowingly, it could affect your partnership. Never wait until it is too late to mention something you need to talk about. Nonverbal Contact

There is a moment when without necessarily saying a word, you have to say something to others, but by using facial expression. With facial expressions, your moments tell tales and as human beings, we strive to say way more about our bodies than what we give ourselves credit for. As a couple, having your body language accessible to each other is important as it can make your partner more relaxed while talking to you. In terms of body language and facial gestures, nonverbal contact does not only have to be, but also other things like physical actions?

• COMMUNICATION SKILLS FOR COUPLES.

For couples, relational skills are skills that require practice, and they are learned over experience. You may be well connected with your partner, but to make your relationship even stronger, communication skills are important.

1. Attention

It is important that you pay full attention to your partner. Hold your mobile phone away from this age of technology and stop calling while your companion is telling you either a joke or revealing a deep secret. It helps them to see that you listen and are keen to hear what they have to tell you as they do that. To confirm to your companion that you are interested in the subject and you are listening, a basic arctic to use is to a node and establish eye contact.

2. Do not interrupt

It can escalate to an argument when your wife talks and you interrupt. Enable both sides to have time to talk so that the counterpart does not believe that they have not been given ample time to articulate themselves. When your partner talks, it is often a little tempting to throw in your feelings, particularly if you feel like your partner missed appointments or two, but keep care of your dreams and give your partner time to finish everything they suggest. When you wait for them to end, a token of appreciation for your companion is often conveyed.

3. Have a neutral space

When in a neutral space, it is always vital to discuss problems. When you plan to address the lack of manhood power of your husband while in bed, a drastic example is that this will make him appear to dislike going to bed and it gives a bad recollection. Such a chat, even if it is at the kitchen table, should be kept somewhere neutral. Taking an argument to a neighbor or the house of a family often lets your companion know as if you are in a safe place for yourself but not easy for them, and this will build space for an argument and not a problem-solving dialogue.

4. Talk face to face

Much as technology offers us contact opportunities that can seem easy and inexpensive, it is advisable to ensure that the conversations are kept face-to-face. Let messaging and phone calls be an outlet for discussing issues that do not require major decisions or issues that are in general contact while in a close relationship. Instead, when faced with something urgent, you will pick a moment when you will face each other and plan it for your chat. Face to face, interaction brings your full attention to each one, and you can even read the nonverbal replies of your companion.

5. Use of "I" statements

A tip to consider to soften the effect of the dispute on your wife should be the use of "I" statements when disputes arise. An example is that "you" did this instead of asking your wife, and it made me angry; you would better say, "I" felt that my emotions were damaged because this happened. This basic strategy allows the two of you not to be in the process of assault and defense.

6. Honesty

Honesty is an uncommon trait, but in developing any stable friendship, it is crucial. You will always tell your partner the truth of what you know when you are truthful, even whether there is a concern that needs to be addressed. Honest also helps you to be able to confess that you have done something wrong and in exchange, instead of making excuses, apologizing for it. Honesty helps to create trust as well as it helps to promote honest and transparent spousal contact.

7. Everything is essential

If it's a big thing or a small thing, never say it's because big stuff started out as little things that were overlooked. It is as important to talk about the small stuff and it will improve the friendship. An instance is when you share your day with your family, your feelings on something or a nice story you've seen elsewhere. For any pair, to the extent where every issue is available for debate, they should be free with each other. There should not be a case where a topic is too uncomfortable or awkward to discuss.

8. Apply 24-hour rule

It is clear that for every couple, not every day is a sunshine day. Days will arrive where things are not going to make sense and there are going to be other days; it's all merry. There are days where you get irritated with your partner, you want to shout and yell at them, and you need to enforce the 24-hour rule at those moments. If the topic doesn't matter to you after 24 hours, so letting it go is a brilliant idea, but if it's really going to hurt you after 24 hours, then you should talk about it after the rage has died down.

9. Physical contact

The sound of the conversation does not matter, but you must retain physical touch. Oxytocin is created when you hug your partner or even just stroke their arm. Oxytocin is the living hormone in intimate partners that fosters intimacy and empathy. Oxytocin also serves as an anti-stress agent that encourages cooperative behavior.

10. Make it fun

When you concentrate on talking about families, financial

matters, challenges and remedies, it is nice to try to make conversation enjoyable. The exchange of funny stories, wishes, and deep talks should require contact or listening to your mate. It is during such periods that stronger emotional bonds are formed, which increase the development of oxytocin and dopamine.

• TIPS FOR EFFECTIVE COMMUNICATION.

1. An intention for connection

You both work on a friendly yet caring friendship so that you can both articulate yourself to the point of your partner knowing you. It is more important to be associated than to find reason or emphasis on being the right one. You are responsive as you reconnect, and you keep in contact with what matters to your partner.

2. Listen more than speaking

The reason God gave us two ears and one mouth is that if we have a discussion, we need to listen more than we say. We seem to forget that when frustration is stirred, we are expected to look we begin to talk more y, or you get into a half-listening state while waiting for your chance to express and make a point. The willingness to listen means that you enter your spouse's world intending to hear them, even though you do not agree with what they suggest.

3. Understand your spouse

She or he will be open to pursuing you as your partner gets to nominate to knowing as if you understand him or her. Generosity, respect, self-control, kindness, and patience are involved in the desire to learn.

4. Understand the need

When someone does something or does something that is due to a personal desire, they believe they have. In addition, where the desire is not communicated orally, you need to listen to hear the wishes of your partner. When you have the ability to recognize a need without clear explanations, a shared understanding is realized.

5. Empathy

Let empathy be at the center of the discussion or conversation. When your partner tells their story and interprets his or her perspective by providing suggestions, you can stop sharing your own related story. She might not be searching for any details at times when your partner shares something, but rather for someone to provide her with a listening ear. Don't want to ignore your partner by either convincing them that your experience is a common occurrence, and many people have experienced it or exposing their dilemma to your spouse is not bad enough relative to what happened to you. Different persons have different stamina for life challenges, because the condition or experience is not linked to your spouse's.

• HOW DOES COMMUNICATION AFFECT RELATIONSHIPS?

To put it plainly, A LOT of ways are the answer. It is highly understandable how relationships are influenced in many forms by something as important as communication. If you are still unsure whether or not it would be worth the effort to put a contact into your relationship, then give a read of these following explanations and let your spirits soar high.

It makes both people feel appreciated,

Validation and love are central needs of humans. No one, especially inside a partnership, likes to feel unappreciated or ignored. Communication is not just a mechanism, which makes it possible for you to communicate what is wrong. When they do, everything right, this practice of letting the other person know how you feel often transcends into appreciating and valuing your mate. Communication thereby means that all people's contributions in a relationship never go unnoticed. By motivating the participants in a partnership to continue working on strengthening their relationship, provides a constructive feedback process.

• Communication is poisonous for miscommunications

Imagine that you send a long and thorough text proclaiming your support for your partner and a quick "okay" is all you get in return. Will you be dismissed? Got hurt? Huh? Angry? Although "okay" in this situation is still an incorrect reaction, a good friendship focused on clear contact will ensure that you do not leap to conclusions? Instead of getting upset, you'd ask if all is all right with your girlfriend. You would politely ask them the explanation behind such a curt reaction instead of accusing them of being heartless. It is only possible to achieve this desire to be cool and not leap to conclusions until you know how the other person interacts in general.

- Your relationship does not have room for arguments

Arguments are also based on a dispute, or a fight for superiority. Connection makes it easier for you to be frank and confident in each other. Thus, when a dispute occurs, you both treat it as a conversation. As compared to you two against each other, a case of you two versus the problem. Strong communication functions as a safe haven to communicate how you feel without fear of judgement or impact. Thus, the friendship no longer feels the need to argue.

- You feel intimate with your partner

It is not all titles and dates that characterize relationships. A relationship's familiarity is judged on how well you know each other and the bond you have. Only if you two are ready to be intimate and open will this relational bond and sense of foster intimacy. By engaging with your partner and making your

165

partner feel understood, this is done. Therefore, you will put your partner far closer to yourself and learn things about them that you have never known before by enhancing intimacy in your relationship.

- You always have context

Sometimes a lack of coordination causes fear and envy. You constantly want to leap to conclusions because you lack knowledge about your other half's emotional state. Not only is this mentality detrimental to your emotional health, it may become suffocating or claustrophobic for your companion as well. However, good and strong communicating with each other allows you to consider the sense in which the other party has said something. It makes you realize the need to allow each other breathing room if possible.

- It prevents unpleasant surprises

Imagine devoting your life to somebody for ten years just to find out that they don't hold your opinions on children? When your partner's lifestyle decisions are in stark contrast to yours, how would you feel? Will you still feel entitled to be mad at your best half if you had never shared what you were angry at? It is akin to buying a surprise package to get serious about a relationship without having spoken properly. What it could reveal, you never know! You let the other party know about your desires and how you feel about those things when talking.

- Communication helps establish trust

We have shown how contact tends to create intimacy, provides meaning for the acts of each other and, most notably, helps to deter fights and misunderstandings. Connection gives you the secret and that is 'mutual confidence' to build a solid basis for your relationship. Your companion needs to be respected and heard. This makes them trust you and your love and see you as a safe haven where, without any inhibition, they can be insecure. When you can expect your companion to have a legitimate explanation behind their actions, it gives you a total peace of mind. Mutual trust protects you from a lot of tension, as you will still feel free to question your partner instead of making conclusions regardless of their unlikely acts.

In conclusion, contact is a mystical package just waiting to be opened, so it can shower you with countless gifts ranging from affection to comprehension, and ultimately create a solid, eternal connection. A communication-reinforced bond is thicker than steel and can withstand any test of time. Therefore, make sure to connect so that the relationship you have always dreamed of can be established.

- **THE EFFECTS OF LONELINESS**

Being alone warps the mind and harms the body physically. A neurological research conducted on the reaction of the brain to rejection and alienation showed that through the anterior cingulate cortex of the brain, the internal distress encountered by the stranger culminated in negative physical symptoms. Higher depression and a weakened immune system result in isolation. Actually, you might get ill from being a loner!

• Make no mistake

Experiencing silence does not involve being actually isolated. Despite sharing a house together, married couples will sense isolation. Something as easy as being distracted with work, according to John Cacioppo, a neuroscientist and psychologist at the University of Chicago, prevents you from communicating with your partner and causes a sense of loneliness. If you and your mistress or missus get bored in the relationship, the same will happen.

You turn on yourself and your own reflections for fun because nothing offers thrilling rewards. Instead, when you are faced with the hideous internal mirror that we call self-doubt, you will find yourself going over your shortcomings. Humans have so much problems dealing with this that we build a phantom presence to cope with it. That is how a belief in the supernatural flourishes, unbelievably.

This is primarily due to the lack of secondary data and

strength that comes from a pack of individuals on which you can rely to validate or refute your own experiences. Each unfamiliar sound we process becomes unclear and leaves the likelihood of phantasms open, the reasoning being that the noise was not made, so who did it? That is why spending time with your partner regularly is supremely valuable. You are legitimately going to go insane if you don't!

• THE LIFE-SAVING BENEFITS OF COMMUNICATION

The explanation of why partner-to-partner contact is so important is that this entity gives you another viewpoint and a way to interpret a situation impartially. When no one is present, you are more likely to make irrational choices to help you process solutions that are more logical. A companion will remind you that keeping your work means keeping a home and food, and even though your boss is a dick, you are still improving your career.

Your special one will give you wisdom all your life. That being said, it will contribute to your downfall if you do not interact with your partner before making major decisions. "What if one day you went home and said, "Honey, I left my job? "Would the response of your partner be positive? I honestly suspect it. The stress pressure falls on them to continue to support when you are hunting for another one. You battle more and may break eventually. In order to stay together, I presume you are reading this, so here is what you can do to stop heartbreak.

Allow time to sit down together and debate major changes rationally. Come to a consensus and fight for the shared values you have. Not only can you save your friendship, however the bonds that bind you will grow.

• The Physical over the Digital

Only because something you said was taken the wrong way via SMS, fights can start quickly. Since your companion is unable to detect the sound of your speech, the way you felt must be inferred. It would lead to an automatic inference that you were pessimistic, just the tiniest touch of vulnerability.

On physical contact and affection, marriages flourish. Remember when I discussed the detrimental side effects that come from isolation before? For lengthy stretches of time, not being touched adds to that. To bring the romantic spark and improve meaningful contact back in your love life, here are a few tips:

There are few things you can do to hold depression at bay and fall in love again, apart from the apparent erotic aspect of physical intimacy.

Following a long and exhausting day, try to give your partner a massage. They would respect the initiative you have shown to make them rest.

Lightly caress a shoulder as you walk by and let your lover know that even though you are not sitting down and experiencing anything together, you are aware about them.

Hug them routinely. Embraces create a sense of comfort and protection. It eventually establishes a strong bond of faith.

PRACTICAL TRAINING TO TRY WITH YOUR LOVER TO IMPROVE THE COMMUNICATION

Compelling communication in marriage can mean the difference between a robust glad association with negligible strain and one that is wild, dangerous, and bound to end. Fortunately, for you, communications habits are something that can be accomplished with enough exercise by anybody.

Also, the great thing of these operations? Both of them should be achievable in the solace of your own house! Peruse on to explore the best correspondence practices and tasks for partners that can help develop relationship or marriage skills while also helping to establish and build trust.

People have been struggling for such a long time to grasp and disentangle the lock to a stable partnership. Scholars and analysts have conjectured a few theories over the years to determine whether a partnership can make it down the walkway, or whether it will drive into a mature age.

Despite diverse emotions, the vital key to demystifying and opening the lock is typically based on correspondence. In the mid-1990s, culture learned that as intrinsic sex traits suspected of miscommunication between partners, "Men are from Mars and Women are from Venus,"

Only a while back, the notion of the "Five Love Languages"

was presented, declaring that all persons interact and perceive desires in an unpredictable manner, giving no attention to sexual identity. Up to this point, humanity is not aware of the off chance that Mars or Venus should book an instructive undertaking, or of the off chance that a skilled translator should be received.

In either case, both social health specialists and partnership masters believe that partners need to connect well in order to continue to see someone happily and positively. Correspondence practices may be used either to restore a disturbed friendship or to preserve a joyous connection. These behaviors can be guided by proficient emotional well-being in an advisory atmosphere or can be done by a couple in their own home.

Exercise 1: "Fireside Chats"

During his presidency, President Franklin D. Roosevelt used informal radio stations to address the people. In front of a cozy chimney, the phrase "fireside visit" was said to conjure visions of one chatting with the President.

In this verbal communication, couples encouraged each other to arrange a "fireside visit" once a week for a short period of 15 days. This practice instructs accomplices to discuss multiple problems through calm and deferential terms. Both interruptions must be eliminated and dismissed, with the emphasis remaining squarely on each other.

"Fireside talks" will discuss either surface or deeper substances or focus, for the most part, on the size of two or three problems. If the spectrum is wide, it indicated that before going on to increasingly warmed, contentious points, a couple begins with more secure" conversations, for example, mainstream culture, world occasions, or enjoyable.

Exercise two "High-Low"

This movement in verbal correspondence helps persons to engage freely, while their accomplice employs mindful listening techniques. This behavior can be used during the last part of the night (for example, during dinner or sleep) and helps a couple to register the most important aspects of their day with each other.

Every accomplice demanded to express the best part of his or her day, his or her "high," and his or her "low." the most baffling part of his or her day. As one accomplice shares, the multiple uses undivided procedures of attention to pass on compassion and empathy.

• Exercise three "Tuning in Without Words"

It is a practice based on both verbal and nonverbal contact. Without interruption, a 3-5 minute clock and one accomplice are given an opportunity to verbalize what they think and feel.

In the meantime, to pass on compassion, understanding, and consolation, the other accomplice will merely use nonverbal techniques. The pair shapes the encounter by communicating about perceptions, emotions, and ideas now where the clock goes off. At that point, each accomplice would shift jobs and get an opportunity to rehearse the two talents.

Exercise four "Eye See You"

It is a nonverbal correspondence activity focusing solely on the eye-to-eye relation. Two seats set each other in a cool, loosening state in this operation. The two players met, without separating or turning around to stay in touch for five minutes. People were encouraged to encourage inside thoughts and feelings to emerge during this action.

Couples were encouraged to evaluate their perception, degrees of solace or anxiety, and significant sensations at the conclusion of the movement. Each participant is given an opportunity to worry about what their accomplice thinks about the relation of the study, and nonverbal messages have run over.

Exercise five "Send Me A Postcard"

It is a trend for communication based on composed correspondence. A vivid postcard with headings is given to the two accomplices to write a note portraying a sadness, an inclination, or a craving. Each accomplice then presented their postcard to "mail" by providing it without verbal exchange to their accomplice. Each accomplice then approached to write a reaction to his or her accomplice's message using another postcard.

Chapter TWO

Creating Trust AND INTIMACY

What is trust?

There is a close relationship between love and trust. Esteem includes showing faith in yourself, your own preferences, and believing others as well. The secret to a partnership is trust. The relationship, without which it would eventually fail, would remain dysfunctional. The principal explanation why relationships split up is loss of trust. The principal explanation why relationships split up is loss of trust.

Why?

In addition, if you do not use trust, it means that you do not have trust that your partner will support you and stay loyal to you. Over all, confidence means you can depend on your partner, support them, and feel happy with them. If no faith occurs, so no contact will take place.

It is the trust that allows us to overcome the unpredictable and complex world in which we live today. With the advent of technology, mobile phones, telephones, text and social networking, it is now much easier for people to connect or spend more time with fellow employers than with family and significant others.

Confidence is crucial for both our personal and professional relationships to be successful. We need faith to evolve over time in order to build significant and enduring relationships.

According to the 2011 Partnerships Metrics Report, the key four variables for friendship breakdowns

- Economic burden

- Interaction challenges

- Varying standards

- Mistrust.

Authentic trust entails moods and thoughts, loving oneself and one's own preferences, respecting others, and the desire to forgive when relationships are broken. If one person is ready and the other person is not it is not easy to gain trust.

Two people who have a strong relationship will express faith in a number of ways, such as:

i. To listen and to help one another

ii. To demonstrate respect and concern

iii. Trusting one another to do what is right for you

iv. Demonstrating mutual concern for boundaries

v. Being helpful to the other

vi. You should feel secure, no matter what happens

vii. To settle disputes in rational ways

viii. Words and actions should match

ix. Not controlling one another or tracking one another

x. Trusting one another irrespective of where they are or who they are with

They can be their true self once an individual has formed a solid, trusting relationship. The creation of confidence takes time, so trust is a choice.

In any partnership, coordination is key. Think of love as a seed that nurtures into a plant just as you grow with another in a relationship as well. The soil is the trust you have in the individual; it gives a seed the room to grow. It will bloom as you plant the seed in good soil. If you grow it in crappy soil, on the other hand, some leaves will spring, but they will die in the end. In the meantime, water is contact. You improve the soil and grow the seed, allowing it to prosper, by spending time with others and opening up to them. A lack of touch, in contrast, will dry out the soil and kill the plant.

In order for a relationship to be stable over the years, you and your partner must work together to retain the trust you have. Do not by betraying mutual trust, allow the foundation to collapse. Making it better by contact that is clear.

• SIGNS THAT SHOW YOUR PARTNER CAN BE TRUSTED

In relationships, confidence is a dicey factor. Often, after we have burned our hands in the past, we want to believe others repeatedly. To benefit from our mistakes is a clever idea, and these signs remind you where you can trust your partner:

1. Open conversations:

He keeps his conversations truthful and open. If he's happy and secure in his conversation, letting his guard down and exposing his deepest secrets and anxieties. This is a sure sign that you should trust him. Let him feel by reciprocating his sentiments that you value him.

2. Admitted errors:

Without inhibiting them, she understands her blunders. She's honest with them, and she's not going to hide an explanation from them. In cases where things can get uncomfortable, she displays integrity as well. Including answering the question 'I'm getting fat?' Answering them sincerely despite knowing that it might not be approved by anyone else.

3. Share your bank account:

Reporting your expenses is one thing, but it's another thing to share your bank account and be honest about your finances. It's just that he trusts you, if he's honest about his financial worth. Trusting him is a warning.

4. You are her top priority:

She puts hers above your needs and interests and makes you feel comfortable. She keeps meeting you and letting people know about your relationship a focus for her colleagues and employers.

5. Responds actively:

Many appear to more regularly disturb the interaction with our companion or have the need to offer advice. Therefore, when your partner listens attentively to what you have to say, indicates that he cares for you and trusts your thoughts, you have to believe him.

6. Real intimacy:

It's not only about sexuality, but the profound bond she's shared with you is illustrated by little things like a good morning hug, holding hands or kissing. Only if she is loyal to you will she carry out these acts.

7. Holds eye contact:

If he reflects on your eyes when listening to you, be assured that he is trustworthy. This shows that he actually has nothing to hide from you. When talking, if he can't meet your eyes, it might mean that he's hiding something from you.

8. She looks after your interests:

If it's about friends, employment, or something else, she takes a special interest in your life's events. She pays attention to the debate and needs to know you better than anybody else does.

9. He meets with your relatives and friends:

He has no trouble communicating with your family and is respectful. For the kids (if any), he has optimistic expectations and treats them as part of his own. You would be lucky to have a person of this sort.

10. She doesn't fear you inspecting her cell:

If she snatches her mobile as you look for that, it's not a good thing in your relationship. This means she doesn't have anything to hide from you as she opens the phone and reads the messages in front of you; that's a positive sign. However, bear in mind that your partner should never be required to show his phone and challenge you to know their passcode. In a partnership that we will explore in subsequent pages, there are certain limits.

11. He is secure and relaxed:

In your relationship, when he is confident, he is his normal self and relaxed around you. If a man becomes dissatisfied in his relationship, it means that he has something to hide. This indicates utter faith in your relationship because you can confess to him without any hesitation or fear of being humiliated.

12. Consistency in action:

She can push her best foot out in the early days, but once you're well into the relationship, you'll find out whether she honors the limits, is blunt and open, and takes care of your needs or otherwise. The person also does not make false pledges or assurances that are impossible to keep. No faith can be asked. It's must be earned. This doesn't come naturally and it takes time and resources to develop trust.

• HOW TO DEVELOP TRUST IN A RELATIONSHIP AND MARRIAGE?

If two people wish to have a fully satisfying relationship, they both need to be able to open up. They both need to be able to be available to each other.

Yet it sounds like exposing your collar to a hungry wolf if you do not trust the other party (or vice-versa), leaving you vulnerable to him or her. This makes no sense because it will, most definitely lead to pain and guilt.

In the middle of a moment, even small things can weaken the trust you've managed to build for months:

- Losing your patience and rendering negative criticism of the other

- Threatening to leave or deceive the other

- Seeking to use an injunction to exploit someone

- Betraying their trust

- When the other doesn't have the back when your help is needed the most

Reciprocal confidence is crucial because you choose to build a relationship that will develop each of you at the highest level. Without it, the relationship will remain in "secure mode" like a system restarting after a sudden shutdown.

Therefore, while you want the other person to feel secure, you know that the kind of relationship you want involves vulnerability. With negligible relations, we're not going to be satisfied. However, both parties will strive to develop trust both within themselves and in the other party to progress past this.

You are human, not supernatural, but you can also do your best to satisfy any of your partner's dreams. In addition, among these requirements that need satisfaction is loyalty. For example, within this zone, if you truly agree to make your marriage work, you will remain committed to your wife. After all, if you are tying the knot with that person, you are actually committed to the relationship at that point.

1. Live as if each day is your final day.

When you have this in your head, you will be ready to die and ready for the judgement of God. When facing temptations, this mindset will help you control yourself. In addition, it would keep you from playing with fire and from staying away from something that does not belong to you, whether it be objects or people.

2. Remember your marriage promises every day and remain loyal to them.

Since it was your only option to tie the knot with your partner, he/she has to be the best one for you and no one else. Therefore, no one can reach the degree of respect you have for your partner, even if you may admire other people. In addition, your acts must be matched to your speech, particularly in terms of your marriage vows.

3. Aside from your marriage vows, keep all your promises.

When you have promised your other half everything, hold that. This would strengthen the confidence of your partner in you, as well as make you more trustworthy. Besides not making second thoughts if you make promises to her/him, your other half will definitely adore your reliability.

4. Only make responsible promises.

Ensure your willingness to keep the commitment first before making a pledge to your best half. Therefore, you ought to thoroughly decide just what you desire for your mate. Never rush to make promises only to please your partner, for the test is to satisfy the commitment you made.

5. Show honesty at all times.

Truthfulness is a positive quality of a person that everybody must strive to develop while creating faith in marriage. It must be your eternal ambition to improve the routine of total accuracy with your best half in all interactions. Lies abolish trust in all relationships, after all.

6. Admit wrongdoings and apologize to your spouse.

Indeed when you confess your wrongdoings, it also hurts. Moreover, it is never easy to muster the confidence to do this, but this is also a way of demonstrating sincerity. In addition, if your partner may not be pleased about what you've done, they're going to learn to respect you for doing it.

7. Be fully sincere with your partner.

It can trigger mistrust in your marriage to keep secrets from your partner. Our pride and ego also prevent us from completely opening ourselves to our spouses. Try including your partner with all the decisions you make to keep this from happening.

8. Never bring about the occasion wherein your spouse would feel that they are very nosy.

For example, you can say exactly where you intend to go in specifics when you leave home and your partner asks where you are going. You should really tell your partner where you are, first, so you don't needlessly think about yourself. It will even nip your spouse's chances of doubting you in the bud.

9. Give your spouse timely information.

It is normal for your partner to want to know the explanation for this when you get home late. So even though being challenged makes you feel so drained and irritated, be careful to quickly provide them with the knowledge to gain trust in your marriage. Under this scenario, it would have been better if you had notified your husband the day before leaving home or called him in advance to avoid being asked when you got home.

10. Try pleasing your spouse whenever possible.

When you work deeply to make your partner comfortable, it makes them know that with nothing to worry or doubt about, they can fully count on you. "When you have the attitude that says, "I agree that inside this union, I will not satisfy all my wishes and wants, however, I can pursue my best potential, demonstrate love and strive to meet the needs of my partner. Your partner will have confidence in you because you remain faithful to your life, so I will share, give and bear.

11. Forgive yourself and your spouse.

Inside your marriage, you will build trust again when you forgive them sincerely. Reconciliation stems from redemption, which paves the way for you to detach and let go of the hurt from your thoughts.

12. Practice humility.

If your companion has wronged you, apologise and ask for forgiveness. Admit your misconduct, express how horrible you feel about everything you did to your partner, how you thought on it many times over, what things you learned from the encounter, and how you expect to improve your behaviour.

Your partner can see the change in your outlook as you have shown from your actions that you are remorseful. It can act as a guide for you to stop making the same mistake by always reminding yourself of the lack of everything you have done.

- **TRUST-BUILDING EXERCISES**

Trust is the foundation of any enduring relationship. Trust is one of the most important things you have to work on, aside from connectivity. Building trust undoubtedly takes some time, and it will take some work to re-establish it. You and your companion are two separate people with different backgrounds, experiences, and opinions on the environment as well as your lives. Therefore, confidence is necessary not only to form bonds with each other but also to help you remain together in the end. A friendship devoid of faith is not going to last. It indicates you and your partner are comfortable in the relationship when reciprocal trust occurs.

In addition, a common explanation of why many relationships cannot last is the lack of confidence. The framework for emotional connection and a clear relation is confidence. Therefore, retaining trust in your relationship is important. Counseling for partners is a perfect way to create trust. If you do not have the time or access to the psychologist of a couple, though, how do you operate on this. Don't think about it because I've got your back! If you want to build more confidence in your relationship, then here are a few activities that you can do as a couple to build trust.

• Your Phones

A common cause of trust concerns encompassed these days

appears to be technology and social media focused. As this is a perfect way for a couple to create trust in the relationship, be frank about the phone as well as social media. This is a very significant area to focus on, especially if a couple is struggling with some problems of infidelity. At times, it may be very difficult to focus entirely on the words of someone else. Alternatively, if you should look at concrete evidence, such as a computer, as it helps restore the trust of your relationship. Decide on an operation relating to your smartphones or social media that you are both familiar with and take it from there. I don't say that you have to keep searching your partner's phone, so if you don't conceal your phone from your partner, it helps to build a certain degree of confidence. For example, it leads to needless distrust when you speak to your partner and keep avoiding a phone call, or stop replying to any texts. Be frank and open with about whom you speak and converse. For the sake of your relationship's wellbeing, focus on gaining some trust.

• Plan Date Nights

Giving up a little advantage is one of the most significant facets of getting some trust in a partnership. We just want to be in charge, because it gives you a sense of peace. You have full power of everything you do because you know that you are the one doing it. Every decision you make belongs to you and you don't count on someone else. However, your wife might begin to hate you if you do not give up a little influence occasionally in the relationship. Do not be in charge, please do not micromanage it. You and your wife would both do your best for a relationship to succeed. One person, while the other does nothing, can not keep making all the effort. Another easy way to give up level power is to schedule your weekly date nights in turns.

• Couple Activities

You are going out of your comfort zone if you try something new. This is not only a fantastic way to shape a closer bond, but also to create morale. An engaging way to develop trust is to participate in a new exercise, such as dancing. Every task that allows you to team up with someone else and needs a degree of teamwork and alignment would be useful. Because you rely on your partner ultimately to perfect a pose or a movement, it induces a sense of reciprocal confidence. Often, this is a nice way to build trust. Apart from this, it is enjoyable and exciting too! Not only can you end up having fun together, you will also have a chance to learn a new talent.

• Vision Board

Creating a vision board is a fun task you and your partner can do together. The vision board consists of the objectives for partnerships and what you want to be like in your relationship. To explain what you want your future to be like, go through different magazines and come up with photos or phrases you might use. When you do this, you will come up with a story about what you want to look like in your future together. The elements that you like more and less of can be quickly decided. This easy exercise encourages you to mutually launch a conversation about the future. It's never easy to have the chat,' and this is a nice way to do it. You may also make a date night out of this operation.

• Your Fears

The trust in your friendship will deepen as you make yourself open and share your fears with a partner. It is all right to be nervous, and you don't always have to put on a mask of being solid. It encourages you to fix any doubts you both have, along with any weakness, by revealing your vulnerability. It offers you a chance to calm down and explore what frightens you. When doing this, make sure that what the other party does is not judgmental or dismissive of either you or your partner. Don't be afraid of being judged. It does not make you vulnerable to talk about your doubts, fears, or insecurities. It makes you just human. Really, it might allow your girlfriend an opportunity to truly appreciate you and your actions. Likewise, it will give you an insight into the thoughts, emotions, and actions of your mate. It becomes easier to fix the root factors of any confidence conflicts in your relationship until all is out in the open.

• SET UP A SENSE OF INTIMACY WITH YOUR PARTNER

Everything in the simple term "intimacy" shows an impression of not being in sex, but being in a position that sets the mindset for it at any rate. Maybe the gatherings involved are not dressed entirely, or maybe they're all crawling closer to each other. At either rate regardless of what you explicitly imagine, it is probably suited to the notion of physically interacting with others, which is a thought that a vast majority of people see as a physical display of prime significance. That's not exactly the right place we're in. Interfacing with another calls for a mix of four kinds of affection, and most of them do not require any form of touch at all.

As suggested by Helene Brenner, Ph.D., behavioral consultant and author of I Know I'm in There Somewhere, association and care comes down to A+ intimacy. "Intimacy is a one-on-one association that includes asynchrony between two individuals," she says. "On the off casual that you need to feel cozy, the principal thing you and your accomplice need to do is stop the various things you are doing and give each other your unified, undistracted consideration."

• Passionate Intimacy

Separate it into three parts to promote enthusiastic intimacy: slow down, make it necessary, and give what is difficult to state. Before you speak, nicely process your emotions, and then while you talk, contextualize your feelings such that you can articulate them as instant and forceful articulations. Think I got injured." "I got terrified." "I love you." "I miss you." "I'm frightened to disclose to you the amount you matter to me." Don't depend on qualifiers to cushion your genuine emotions; instead, get to the base of your unfiltered honesty correct. Alternatively, more importantly, just allow yourself to be defenseless.

• Mental Intimacy

As a meeting of the psyches, conceive of emotional intimacy: it is delightful, testing and conceivably invigorating (envision two little cerebrums in Paris, tasting red wine by candlelight). "For certain individuals, this is incredible mind and repartee they love ricocheting off one another, testing one another," Dr. Brenner says. "[Mental intimacy] can likewise be extraordinary discussions about films or a play you saw, or the vocation you both are in or the makes that issue you."

Have a topic to return to with the accomplice who energizes both of you in this way. Perhaps it's an undertaking you need to begin together or an enthusiastic passion you share comparable to tennis or rock-climbing. Ensure that you spend vital energy-connecting steps in what mentally animates you, "Ensure you invest critical measures of energy connecting in what animates you intellectually," What's more, there's no downside to a little lively competition, so have a go at pre-packaged games against each other to the point that you're decently evenly organized.

• Physical Intimacy

Many people make their supreme strength the form of intimacy, and it's not necessary! Physical contact will possibly be the key avenue for the love you both speak well and that's exceptional.

Basically, physical intimacy is about unwinding into it, engaging in its development, getting into the occasion, and expressing what feels better, offering, getting, and connecting. It's all about association, passion, pleasure in sharing and receiving, and affection," Dr. Brenner says. "Ask for what feels best. "Request what feels better. Go for what feels better."

What's more, you'll feel connected with these kinds of intimacy at play, trust me. Because you're aware of the various kinds of intimacy, look at the contrasts between love and attraction. Similarly, how to impart your fantasies to your S.O. It will help privacy. It essentially brings different things to different people. You may feel close to a date when watching a movie together, when you are watching a movie together.

That's how closeness means different things to different

people. Your own definition of closeness may be shaped by your inclinations, type of correspondence, or preferred ways to being more comfortable with others.

There are different kinds of closeness, moreover. Think of the kinds of closeness and make sense of whether closeness is meant for you. Closeness falls into a few distinct classifications, including:

• Passionate

The element that allows you to tell your friends and relatives close to home something that you would not discuss with strangers is enthusiastic closeness. Imagine trusting your guard to protect it when you realize that you can trust others, you have a sense of confidence enough to cause your dividers to break.

• Physical

Touch and proximity between bodies is about physical closeness. It can involve clasping hands, snuggling, kissing, and sex in an intimate relationship. To have physical closeness, the relationship does not need to be sexual or emotional. A tight, warm hug is a case of physical closeness with a partner.

• Experiential

By spending quality resources with someone and developing deeper over daily premiums and workouts, you build experiential closeness. There's nothing comparable to how you interact with someone over your mutual "Round of Thrones" relationship or during a fun Monopoly session.

• Otherworldly

Otherworldliness means different things to different individuals, so profound closeness can therefore vary. Otherworldliness is as a rule, about confidence in something outside the actual sphere of presence. The conviction can for example, be in a greater power, inhuman spirits, or a more noteworthy purpose. Profound closeness can seem like sharing a traditional attribute such as benevolence, being on a similar basis

• Trust

You must have the option to trust them in order to share individual parts of yourself, such as your most degrading privileged insights or your darkest feelings of anxiety.

Showing somebody else that you're trustworthy will also make them feel closer to you.

• Acknowledgment

You know that when you feel like a person accepts you for

who you really are, you have set up a closeness. At the point when you first meet someone you can stress that they may hear your music playlist "extravagance" and think you are peculiar. In any case, when closeness grows, you can shake out to your preferred groups of kids and trust that regardless of how weird you are.

• Genuineness

Feed one another with genuineness and closeness. You can't get one without the other on a daily basis.

You feel comfortable asking your accomplice just how you think to a small degree because you've grown too attached to each other. What's more, you will grow much closer every time you speak up in a similar way. If you need to discuss something in person, you can know that your accomplice is willing to listen.

• Wellbeing

Opening the darkest, most honest self with someone else will put you in a very vulnerable position.

That's why when you meet another human; you can usually get your guard up. You also don't have the vague understanding if they're going to help you, as you should be. In these respects, closeness means feeling a sense of confidence enough to face the risk of putting yourself out there, realizing that the other person cares enough not to let you down.

• Sympathy

It's a stunning propensity to feel cared about, right?

After a horrible breakup, you know your BFF will be there for you. You acknowledge that your sister won't want seven days to pass without knowing how you're doing. With compassion between humans, forgiveness and understanding will only occur.

Empathy is a special portion of thought about the prosperity of each other.

• Friendship

Thinking of each other is a single act, but by showing that you give it a second thought, you also create closeness. Friendship can be tangible, comparable to a handshake between sweethearts or a hug between a parent and a young child, but it doesn't have to be.

Here and there is affection in the subtle ways you appear to each other, similar to when your partner goes through t

• Correspondence

There is a reason why excellent correspondence is most often called as the path to a healthy relationship. You will develop a strong understanding about each other when you bring in an attempt to tune in to others and show to them how you actually feel. What's more, the more you see each other the happier you get.

Closeness typically does not arise automatically, it must be established.

You're not going to get up one morning and state, "At this point, we're personal." Important! "

Closeness is increasingly comparable to a consistency that you continue to build for some time. The more time you spend exchanging encounters and feelings, the more elements you need to interact with to assemble closeness. It normally doesn't just come. You can have some concern or even apprehension for closeness to the structure.

That is justifiable; taking into account the closeness expects you to be helpless and put trust in others if there is a chance that they may cause you to fall down. It will take a long time to take a gamble with them or some other person again on the off casual that someone has ever abused your confidence.

• Convey About Your Emotions

For someone that does not know that you are creating any painful memories, it is hard to build trust. If you have a sentimental accomplice, you might confess to them that it is tough for you to allow others access, then you take a shot at it.

You should also express what you are nervous about and where your feelings of dread come from on the off possibility that your feeling is sufficiently pleasant. It is OK to mention to people in your life what you need from them to get a sense of confidence throughout your relationships.

• Get Proficient Assistance

We will also be able to use some encouragement to confront our feelings of trepidation now and then. Mental health specialists such as a specialist can provide that. An expert can also advise you: making sense of how the fear of closeness started.

Working through critical challenges such as accident understands whether the most productive way to retain closeness in any relationship is included in a psychological wellbeing situation such as avoidant character dilemma or gloom. It is common for connections to become stagnant after some time as life disrupts the general flow, and you slip into a standard that is not as daring as when you first met.

Here are a few thoughts of every relationship to initiate or reignite closeness. Make it a point to express your gratitude. Set aside any effort to note what you acknowledge about them to the next party. Show your appreciation, which may manifest as endowments, gifts, or a much obliged." simple.

Put out an effort to find out about each other. It may seem like the "riddle" is no longer, because you have known anyone for such a while.

Chapter THREE
Dialogue for Couples

One of the most powerful ways of contact is dialogue between couples in a committed love relationship. The same way that yoga encourages people to bond with their own selves is the same way that conversation allows partners to have a closer interaction with each other. The consequent back and forth debates and blame games are never safe when partners disagree. Not too many people face up to being the source of conflict in marriages at the end of the day. The finger is often pointed at the other party in most situations. Dialogue serves as a tool in which couples sit down, have sober and rational conversations in a manner that reconciles and sets the stage for going on towards a healthier relationship. The following parts shed more light on conversation and its positive influence on partners.

Efficient Dialogue Tips

1. Active listening

Persons, it is normal to listen to others, but they are not present. He or she may be overwhelmed by their feelings on something that is happening in their lives, or he may be excessively attentive to the strong emotions that his partner is expressing. People are much more prepared to provide defensive input when debating than to listen to and consider what the other person is doing. That may be the reason why arguments take longer that storytelling. In conversation, the greatest challenge is that we do not listen to understand, but we listen to answer.

Active listening skills include making a deliberate attempt to calm down and listen with the openness of both the mind and heart. It is a lot better said than done, but the most important thing is that you want to do it. If you find that you are not patient for a discussion or that there is so much to deal with on your head, you must arrange the interview later so that it can be effective. Often, since the speaking is more like an assault than just a discussion, someone may fail to listen, so someone gets irritated and aggressive.

If you can share suggestions or actually reaffirm what you have heard the other person say, as an indication of your comprehension, constructive listening is easier. A clear awareness that you are being understood and noticed is one thing that is promoted to positively change the dynamic. It does not happen instantly to comply with what the conversation is revealing, but aim to demonstrate that you get the viewpoint of the other party to the best of your abilities. Being good at listening effectively in a conversation is a talent that takes practice. Being willing to do so further helps you to get better at it and makes it simpler as well. Note, conversation or conversation is not an option but a need in a partnership.

2. Edit criticism Criticism

When speaking to your mate, it is a personal aim to stop personal critique. Like eye rolling, you must refrain from put-downs, threats, and derogatory body language. They automatically get aggressive when you criticize others. Criticism can contribute to inhibiting the listening process in the long term, thereby triggering a rise in appetite and bruised feelings.

3. Be gentle

The sound of the speech appears to modify during a debate. It would take a long way to help create a constructive dialogue if you will sustain a soft, polite language that is neither passive nor aggressive. It is helpful if you have anything that worries you, if you can bring it up politely and without guilt.

4. Seek first to understand vs. being understood

In addition, before you engage in any discussion, awareness should be one of the crucial goals. It is the intention of any person to be understood at any given moment, since successful relationships require the comprehension of others. Human nature can drive you to find a listening ear, so by focusing your mind on knowing the other person, aim to change your concentration.

5. Ask open-ended questions

You ought to take part in transparent topics that increase awareness and attention. When a conversation is all worked up, it helps to ease the pressure and add a distraction.

Stay calm: To keep the conversations as private as possible, do you are hardest. It is prudent for you both to take a break in case things worsen and then reconsider later when you feel less emotionally powered. Be mindful not only of your mate, but also of yourself when you talk to him. Make sure you stay reasonably cool and do not intensify the fires of psychological distress.

6. Share appreciations

A healthy friendship is meant to make you feel loved and appreciated. It is good if you can pause for a moment to let the other party see what you appreciate about them while holding a conversation. In a friendship, it is healthy if you can make five times as many positive comments as the negative ones you make. It adds to a number of good emotions as you express gratitude. People think and relate best when they are feeling confident about themselves.

- **STEPS FOR INTENTIONAL DIALOGUE**

• Step 1: Mirroring

Mirroring is the condition in which you should be able to listen without distorting his or her emotions or emotions about your partner. Mirroring helps the companion, without judging, to convey himself or herself. Here are steps for a good exercise of mirroring:

You need to let your companion know the particular message you want them to hear. You need to tell your partner, "I feel hurt when you do not listen to me whether you're hurt, or you're not happy with a particular situation.

Then your companion should be able to mirror your message to decide whether they have correctly heard what you said.

You should clarify the message again and then let them mirror you before you believe the signal is well heard if you happen to find like your companion has not understood you well.

You will now complete your message and your thoughts when you know your message is home, so that your companion does not respond to incomplete messages.

Enable your partner to have summaries of what you said to check that they got what you said.

You will now move on to the next stage after you determine that your message is clear.

• Step 2: Validating

One part is listening, then paying attention to what your companion says and thinking it is another distinct matter. Steps for the validation exercise include:

In order to confirm it it is not a requirement for your companion to comply with your claim.

A communication is validated using affirmative expressions such as, "I can see what you're saying, and I can understand why you're saying that the use of those sentences makes it clear to your partner that approval has been earned by his or her message.

Our partner wants to make sure you know your message's authenticity is okay, so you can move on to the next level.

• Step 3: Empathizing

What follows is empathy following the expression of a thought. Empathizing with the emotions of the partner helps promote intimacy and an intimate bond.

Exercise Empathy.

"I can see that you are feeling…"I can see that you feel...

"Let your partner confirm what they feel so that you do not work with assumptions in order for you to be able to know you are actually on the same page. You have to ask, "Is that what you feel? "You should explain the post, then.

After moving through all these steps, you can easily switch to the next level.

• Step 4: Giving the Gift

You should request a minor yet emotionally meaningful change at this stage. With a behaviour change, the only way to change something unpleasant or hurting is to transform something in the form of a reward; you can apply for a behavior change.

The gift exercises

"So that it does not come out as a command, the gift exercise should be very polite. You can start with Can I ask you for something? "Example; "Can I get you a hug? Can you give me a kind word? "

If your companion will cooperate, it is all right. When you get to this point, it is enjoyable because it yields positive progress in your relationship. You need daily practice to do this and it will feel a bit of an uphill challenge at first.

In your busy lives, you should spend particular time as a couple, maybe even just once a week, where you come together and practice deliberate dialogue. You will find that it is getting much more fun after you have done so for a while as it leads to creating intimacy between the two of you.

• DIALOGUE MISTAKES THAT COUPLES MAKE

1. Assuming that talking more is the solution.

A common saying notes that the hallmark of a good relationship is excellent communication, but the fact is that success in a relationship is not just the product of excellent communication. The effects can be the opposite of pleasure when you talk so long. For women, speaking has a way of helping them feel a bond with the other person, but the case might not be the same for men. When you develop a friendship, it is very important that you find the right ways to communicate before talking. Communication can cause feelings of disconnection and pain. Together, you will do a joint task, and by recognizing the contributions of your mate, you end up building greater connectivity that is the prerequisite for good contact.

Try to understand the primary speech style of your relationship and persons have distinct languages of love or ways to better convey love. Behavior talks louder than words to other people, but if you are dating somebody that sends you so many compliments but does not support you with the house chores, so you are in complete disconnect.

Frequent talking is constructive and required. From studies, for at least five hours a week the happy couple chat with each other. It is important that the communication be in accord. You have to make sure you are doing it productively while you are in a debate.

2. Expecting your partner to read your mind

I am sure you have been hoping for your partner to do something you so desperately wished to do but your partner disappointed you because they did not have an idea. No human is great at reading the minds of another person. You can never believe that your partner is outstanding and that they accept what you do or what you need or want. You may find that your partner wants help with housework in a busy environment, but if you do not discuss it, they may not lend you a hand. Your husband might see a sink full of dishes and think that somehow you want to do it in a special way, so he can stroll away happily and watch television while you whine about a vain, lazy, inconsiderate husband inside yourself. Any presumption is literally a killer in contact.

3. Giving in and not saying what you need or think

Do not encourage the feelings to be inactive in the name of satisfying the other person by being opposed to disputes. It can only preserve the peace for a little time if you are a conflict-avoidant. The order will eventually erode your satisfaction for some time, which will then be visible in the relationship.

A researcher writes and claims that a two-way path is a perfect marriage. You are traveling on a one-way street without any contact if you do not have any arguments or one hand is still controlling the flow. That is not anything to applaud.

4. Harping on issues

In their defense, once you have a partner who is not able to let go of toxic conversations and is constantly repeating reckless lessons, it lets the other partner quit. Yapping would not contribute to any dialogue, which is positive or efficient. When a companion perseveres with this action, he merely sees an unseen symbol of "keep going" You become an ignorant, attentive professor who makes strong monologues that end in defensive silence. After some time, you will find that nothing is being resolved, and since both sides are becoming tired and suspicious, the partnership will begin to deteriorate.

The pattern of contact falls on the declining side at those periods. A quick mention of the other party's making us chat will make your partner want to run and hide. It causes disconnection and extends the intimacy distance as you build and work through a habit of talking to someone and you forget it is about talking to someone. With a constructive intention, you might have nice remarks, but what counts is the manner of execution. It automatically switches to harping whether they are like a bullet point list of ideas or a stern monotone monologue without intermissions. Harping plunges someone into silence, which may have little constructive effect on the relationship.

5. Not considering things from the other person point of view

There is no better way to get to a stage where you have built a healthier, more upfront, or know the right way to connect with your mate. The other significant factor is making an attempt from the point of view of your companion to consider things. Empathy is one of the empathy qualities you need both individually and professionally to learn. Compassion is not about deciding to particular problems with your partner, but being on the same page with your partner.

- **STEPS TO HELP COUPLES OVERCOME THE RELATIONSHIP BARRIERS**

Falling in love is one thing, but remaining in love is something completely different. Each partnership can experience various stumbling habits, and learning how to cope with them is important. To solve the obstacles, talks must be had that can be of support.

By focusing on the good old days when your love was blossoming, go back to the start of your friendship. Take your time and share the happy memories of the time you fell in love, and the development of this young love was all your concern.

By talking to each other about your emotions, opinions, and the state of your relationship, analyze your present relationship. Not only do you need to reflect on the positive, but take time to consider the negative emotions as well. Take the time to write down your responses so you can post them. Your emphasis can be on stuff like listing the reasons you believe that you have improved, naming the things you miss most from the early stages of your relationship, listing the things you find like you get upset when your wife does them.

Set up the starting point for drifting. Much, if not all, of the relationship issues begin very slowly, then they build up traction with time especially if they go unresolved. It allows you to support to avoid new stumbles from showing up as you realize the minor disconnects that you did not have the opportunity to attend.

"You can consider questions such as, "Remember a time when you thought your partner was drifting apart? You should be able to identify the explanation why you were unable to cope with the previous obstacle. If you look at it closely, you will find that the framework for an earlier dilemma that does not get a solution must play a role in your current case. More often than not, a circumstance has instilled distrust because the answer has not been good.

Find out the things you need from each other by talking to each other about your desires and aspirations to create a reawakening of your affection.

When you fail, chat about the best ways that you want to tackle challenges in the future. Based on the fresh appreciation that you have about each other's wants, wishes, worries, weaknesses, and skills, you can render partnership vows. Resolutions should be as easy as letting your wife know that you are injured.

• DIALOGUE AS RELATIONSHIP TRANSFORMER

In essence, talking is the realistic objective of developing human and political skills that help solve problems. A conversation is a questioning and stimulating form of discourse opposed to a debate whereby the parties concerned attempt to split up their opinions and ideas. It centers on providing an atmosphere for dispute resolution while a dialogue is involved.

On the right, getting a conversation is a skill. However, a well-crafted description that is rigorous and comprehensive is the very process of communication. A conversation can differ in the following ways from other modes of communication processes:

A negotiation is between parties who are willing to reach a compromise, when dialogue is what parties are not yet prepared to discuss, but wish to alter a conflictual, unhealthy, or distractive relationship.

Instead of bargaining for territorial goods or rights, negotiation will alter a partnership by providing a new framework for reciprocal respect and cooperation.

A dialogue will require new content to emerge that is popular to all parties and will not allow for a situation in which one party prevails over the other.

It can be a systemic tool for change when conversation is continuous. The length of the process of discussion varies from the essence of the problem; some can be brief, while others can be lengthy. When the actors are in charge of a dialogue, it is more fully personal and the people involved will be willing to participate in the interest of peace.

• OVERCOMING DIALOGUE BARRIERS

A scenario that appears simple ends up being incredibly awkward for the other party when coping with interpersonal difficulties, and vice versa. It is often a point of consideration whether the reason for holding a difficult talk is the success of the dispute or the admission of the error. In any awkward conversation, however, two major obstacles are present:

The fear of the response of the other person

Emotional pain that rises through the debate

• Barrier 1: Fear of the other person's response

Nothing is more irritating than having a conversation with someone territorial, sensitive, and a hothead, as much as you would like to make peace. You would gladly want to escape someone else's frustration, regardless of who you are, especially if the source is in a problem-solving courtroom. The only value of fear is that fear is embedded in the mind; it is made up of intuition and not something, that has happened before or now. Imagine the scenario where you have not heard the conversion but you are concerned about how everyone will react.

The theory behind fear is that you take too much time to fear and stop a discussion merely because you believe the other entity is going to be offensive or defensive. It is also to your desire that when they come to have a conversation with you, you could give them a memo asking them not to be hostile. Naturally, the brain has been programmed to want certainty, so we do our hardest to look for what we expect. If you have a relationship with someone from a certain moment when you might have been grappling with another problem, so you have an idea of tossing him or her out. Since you have an understanding about how they will respond to you, you can take advantage of it and brace yourself for the discussion. Although awareness might sound like a smart thing for you to stop conversation at the same time, if you take it on the positive side, it may help you develop trust knowing what is waiting for you. It gives you a blank page in the case where you have no experience with the other person, which brings us to the second obstacle called emotional distress.

• Barrier 2: Emotional discomfort

It creates a lot of drama in your brain because you have a picture of how the other person is going to react. When I made an error that was so accidental, it reminded me of my youth, and what I could keep worrying of was how I would get punishment all day long. I spent a lot of time worrying about that statement. I feel that the idea of the sentence, looking back, was so much more traumatizing than the sentence itself. Fear of punishment made me so worried that if I made a mistake in the morning, I could end up having a full day of worry and distress. My parents will come home at times after a long day of trauma and say, "It is okay; we understand that it wasn't your fault." Looking at it now, I know and resent how much time I spent nursing my problems.

It is not their reaction that you dread most in such a situation, but how you would feel depending on their response. For starters, you will feel bad if the subject cries, or you will get upset if the object gets defensive. What makes you feel sympathy for the other party and wish you could stop the discussion is the idea of someone crying while talking to you. Around the same moment, the fact that you are trying to talk to someone upset, but whether they are crazy or defensive, you are equally not aware about their responses instills an anxiety that makes it easier for you to stop the conversation than face it.

• HOW TO OVERCOME DIALOGUE BARRIERS?

- Mindset 1:

See the portrait of a capable and ready human in your own eyes. The entity you are now referring to as an adversary or a very irrational and violent person should not be identified to you. Believe in your mind that this person is able to not only listen to me but also to understand me if I introduce myself well. Have faith and put your ideas right and in a way that is presentable. Note, they do not have to say you are right, but what you are asking for is that your thoughts are confirmed.

- Mindset 2:

There may be different options than the one that you have on your head. You ought to be open to alternatives. As long as you are trying to think up stories about how they are going to react, you still need to leave some space for the likely possibilities. It helps you to feel comfortable when you are open-minded, particularly when interacting with someone with whom you already have a background. In your defense, the open-mindedness generates when you have not aligned yourself to a specific result. You're going to have to give them a chance; if it doesn't go well you're going to brave and say I tried, if it goes well you're going to rejoice fairly and say I'm happy I did it.

- Mindset 3:

All is accountable for their emotional replies. For whatever emotional reaction you get from individuals, you need to learn how to feel relaxed. By trusting that any feeling they get belongs to them and not to you, you will empower yourself. Let the people you are concerned with take absolute responsibility for their feelings. If you have a talk with someone and they tend to weep, instead of handing him or her over a handkerchief or other tissue, do not encourage sympathy to take over. The person you are having a conversation with will become too protective and violent in another incident. You need to take a deep breath, send them a serious look in their eyes and remind them to continue with the discussion later, as much as it is bothersome and frightening at the same time, mostly because you do not know how worse they will react when they get upset. If necessary, remind them to let you know so they will let you know when they are calm and able to talk about the issue. You will close the possibility of them claiming that you want to talk about something as you do that, but they are not prepared to talk about it. A thing to remember is that you do not need to take care of them what you need to do is be in charge of their thoughts without having sympathy for yourself.

CHAPTER FOUR

The Role OF Empathy in a Relationship

To bloom and evolve, a healthy partnership needs various features. In providing a solid establishment in a relationship, values such as respect and confidence are important; but sympathy is essential in forming the deeper relationship between you and your loved one.

One study reveals that in sentimental organizations, the view of feeling understood or shown compassion is a critical portion of fulfillment. Analysts believe that knowing our emotions helps us to accept these feelings all the more often and empowers us to potentially proceed with additional rewarding lives (Cramer and Jowett, 2010).

The desire to consider and name others' sentiments. In a given case, we should have the option to peruse and interpret how our accomplice feels. Think if the accomplice can potentially cope with a certain moment and how they can be impacted because of getting the option to recognise the tendency that the other party is feeling.

The ability to carry up the points of view of others. We can also have the possibility of viewing the situation from their eyes, distinguishing the feelings of others. Make use of what you think of them. Understanding that they sound like this. Everyone suddenly sees the moment. Everyone has an opposing perspective, and long-haul ties help us to consider how our accomplice can react to different circumstances.

What Is Empathy?

Individuals prefer to associate compassion with empathy. However, it is important for you to know the difference between the two. Getting compassion for others means feeling love or sadness for them while faced with any tragedy. Getting empathy involves being able to understand their emotions and express them.

It is not unprecedented for persons to argue with each other about things. All has beliefs and feelings of their own. It is necessary, though, to value the emotions of the other person and not attempt to rail over them with your own. In a friendship, that is exceptionally so. You have to develop a sense of humanity to endure the values and emotions of the other person. Empathy would help you to do so and build a good relationship with your partner.

☐ Influence of Empathy in a Relationship

Getting empathy for your partner is vital to you, and they can do the same for you too. You would be able to sense what they are doing in a way because you can empathize with another human. For one, when they are happy, you can understand their pain or feel happy. If you cultivate sensitivity within yourself, you will be able to perceive the feelings of your partner even when they begin to shift. This is important in making you to appreciate each other and when they need it, have assistance. Getting empathy will allow you to become more empathetic.

It is important to cultivate compassion in yourself as it will make you want to assist your companion in their time of need and provide them with the support they need. You would not be able to show sympathy for them either if you fail to have empathy for the other person. This is because you may struggle to consider their feelings and therefore therefore fail to react properly.

People who lack empathy are typically the ones who are cruel to others, according to several reports. They struggle to understand how the other person feels influenced by their comments and acts. These persons lie to themselves and fail to take responsibility for their actions. Rarely do they show regret for harming another person. Many days, individuals are so caught up in themselves that they ignore their nature to cultivate empathy. If it is at work or at home, this will have a negative influence on all their relationships in life.

Currently, empathy is at the core of a happy friendship. If it loses empathy, the friendship will fail to thrive. Without empathy, you will show understanding, and this will influence the relationship you share with your mate. Empathy is like a bridge between two people who have opposite emotions, opinions, or perspectives. Empathy can come in three ways.

Cognitive empathy is when you can look at stuff from the viewpoint of another person but can not sense his or her thoughts. It will help you to grasp a situation that the other person is facing.

Emotional empathy helps one to feel what is felt or believed by the other person. It enables you to interact more emotionally with the person.

A combination of both cognitive and emotional empathy is caring empathy. It helps you to see stuff from the viewpoint of the other person and empathize with their feelings.

Compassionate empathy is something you need to cultivate within yourself to a larger degree. There may also be a detrimental effect on perceptual or emotional empathy. For example, someone to exploit someone for his or her benefit may use it. Yet you can have remorse and be less likely to try to hurt anyone with compassionate empathy. If you have compassionate understanding, before you do something, you will think twice and be more considerate of the emotions of your companion. You can empathize and attempt to keep things tidy if you know that your companion is irritated or upset when the room is dirty. Your empathy will make you become a strong companion, and they will value your efforts. With respect, kindness and understanding, loving empathy can help you respond to your partner.

• HOW TO DEVELOP EMPATHY

You should attempt to nurture empathy within yourself now that you understand the value of it. The following measures will assist you to become more caring.

1. Increase your self-awareness.

You will therefore be able to perceive this in others as you become more attuned to your own feelings and thoughts. If you are upset by something, you will know that it might also hurt another person. When your partner is saying or doing something, take care of how you feel and think. Do not be too immersed in yourself and learn to manage the way you react.

2. Practice self-empathy.

When you can't sympathize for yourself, you will refuse to empathize with your partner. When you are going through a tough time, you need to pay heed to your own feelings and appreciation. It should always be a priority to take care of yourself. In an effort to take care of your partner, do not cheat on self-care. You will be more able to care about them if you take care of yourself too. Without terrible situations, you should face your problems. It will allow you to face all that comes your way by staying cool and poised.

3. Pay attention to body language.

Be mindful of the vocabulary of your body and learn to observe that of others, too. The gestures, voices, and diverse motions of a person will say a lot about their feelings.

4. Observe nonverbal cues.

It is always more revealing how a person says things than what they are thinking. The nonverbal signs can help to describe their emotional reality.

5. Develop the habit of listening well.

If you do not really listen to what they are doing, you would not be able to empathize with others. Pay heed, and be a good listener, to the details. When they talk, stop interrupting anyone. Offer them an opportunity to be able to express themselves. So many individuals are more focused on communicating than on listening. In all times, give your partner sincere consideration. Do not worry on finding a way to protect yourself, even though you disagree. Pay heed to what they mean and attempt to grasp their point of view.

6. Look for the positive aspects of your partner and your relationship.

You affect your capacity to empathize healthily when you dwell too much on the negative. Instead of always thinking of the poor, start taking care of the good stuff.

7. Avoid being judgmental or doubting what the other person says.

Listen with an open mind and heart. Do not worry too hard on trying to give advice or asking them what to do or not to do. When an individual shares their dilemma, they trust you and seek help. You should concentrate on listening rather than attempting to fix the problem. Hold back your own thoughts and beliefs and reflect on what the other person feels and needs from you. It will discourage you from behaving mindfully towards your wife by getting so embroiled in your viewpoint.

To create a feeling of appreciation for your partner and others use these guides. The way you interact with people will make a lot of difference, and that will strengthen your interactions with them positively.

• HOW TO COMMUNICATE WITH EMPATHY

You have to start talking with it in mind so that you learn a bit more about empathy. If you are someone who tries to find the right words to say, it might encourage you to sort out the following statements.

Acknowledge the suffering in your mate.

In all stages, it is important for you to understand how they feel. When you interact with their suffering or pain, they will feel encouraged.

You may use the following sentences:

- "I'm sorry you've got to go through this."

- "I hate that you had this happen."

- "I wish I could turn things around for you and make it easier."

- "This must be difficult for you."

- "This must be a difficult situation for you, I can see."

• Share your feelings.

When you do not know what to say or do, you should be honest and admit it. Imagining what the other person Is going through is not always easy. Share your feelings with your companion and let them know you are trying.

You may use the following sentences:

- "I wish I could improve things."

- "For you, my heart hurts."

- "I can't imagine how difficult this will be for you."

- "I'm truly sad it happened to you."

- "I'm sorry you feel like this."

• Show your partner that you are grateful when they open up to you.

People find it hard to open up to someone and to be insecure. More often than not, at some stage, their trust has been broken. In addition, you need to be thankful and show that, as they want to believe you. Show your partner that you value their feelings and feelings being shared with you. Acknowledge how hard it can also be for them to do this.

You are required to use the following sentences:

- "I'm happy you've shared this with me."

- "I'm glad you're saying this to me."

- I can imagine how painful it would be to learn about this. Thank you for sharing yourself with me.

- I appreciate that you are trying to work hard on our connection. I know that you are trying, and it gives me hope.

- Thank you for showing faith in opening and me up. For you, I want to be there.

• Show your partner that you are interested.

If your partner is going though, you have to take an interest in. It can be daunting to go through tough times alone. You have to reach out to convince them you are there to help them. Show them that whatever they have to say, you are interested in listening. Do not give too much direction or too many views. Just be a polite listener.

You are required to use the following sentences:

- "If you want to talk, I'm here for you."

- How are you talking about anything that has been happening lately? "

- "Are you OK?" Is there anything you like to talk about? "

- "I think you're feeling like Am I right? Did I misunderstand?"

- "What has this been like for you?"

• Show encouragement.

You have to be encouraging when your loved one is going through a difficult time. However, in the right way, you ought to go through this. Do not want to address the issue or offer unsolicited advice. Only help them to feel happier and inspired in a way that makes they feel. Show them you care for them and you believe in them.

You may use the following sentences:

- "You are strong, and I believe this is what you can get through."

- Still by your side, I am. You're never meant to feel alone.'

- "I'm proud of everything you did."

- "You matter, and you should never call it into question."

- "You're a very talented individual."

• Show support.

Actions at times matter more than sentences. To prove your partner you are there to assist and help them in some difficult times, you should take some easy acts. To make them feel better, you should give them roses. For them, you should do any chores. Only do whatever you think they're going to enjoy, and it will make their lives a bit simpler.

You are required to use the following sentences:

- "The "I want to do it for you.

- "Always "I am here to listen.

- Is there anything that I can do right now for you? "

- Is there any chance that I could help? "

- "Tell me what you need to have."

However, in the end, when it comes to sympathy, there is no set script. You have to be more attuned to the requirements of your mate and behave likewise. Half the job for them is about listening and being there.

• Show Your Partner You Appreciate Them

A lot of us appear to over time take our friends for granted. We love them, and we know they're doing a great job for us. However, after all that they do for us, we neglect to thank and respect them. When you think about it, you're actually doing it too. This is why I have devoted this segment to learning more about how your partner can express gratitude.

A lot of you can shirk it off and say that you dislike expressions of love that are apparent or public. You can tell you love your partner and they already know it so it doesn't have to be seen all the time. But this is where you're misguided. Would you like it more if they showed their gratitude when you do something good with your spouse, or is it only enough that you know that they love it in their hearts? Everyone wants a little show of thanks and love. When they see this extra effort from their mate, it makes them feel good and happy. Remember this when you think of how you can act with your partner: How do you expect them to behave and treat you? In addition, are you still doing the same? For all, there is still a common rule of thumb: "Do to others as you would have them do to you." You should treat individuals the way you wish to be treated too. So, if you like a bit more appreciation, why not do your wife the same thing?

Typically, major romantic gestures get all the hype. They will be appreciated, but not all of them are that important. If you remember to be persistent with your efforts, minor movements will play a lot greater role in the long term. It would all add up if you make a point to keep reminding your companion that you value them. Sending a huge bouquet once a year does not cut it. The little movements you make on a daily basis will serve to make your relationship ever better and it will reflect the passion and devotion you have for your partner.

Couples have argued in a number of surveys about the fact that they believe their partner doesn't respect them enough. They still feel like they are pouring a lot of time into their partner, but they get no evidence of gratitude or acknowledgment for it. This can be stressful for the partner, depressing, and leaving them disappointed. A fair way will go by expressing a little gratitude. You can find that all of you are much happier together when you start showing your partner affection, and the passion feels rekindled.

• Thankfulness is key to any relationship.

Recognizing others makes them enjoy what they do and they find it has a positive influence on their life. It makes it easier for them to think of themselves in a positive way, helping them to proceed with fresh energies, improving the friendship.

Things are what they are; how can you know when you felt unappreciated by your partner?

A few indicators may indicate that the difficulties in your relationship might be ignored and your wife thus feels undervalued:

- They get into battles over apparently negligible information.

- They have been behaving increasingly emotional of late.

- They don't enjoy talking as much to you as before.

- They no longer want your opinion.

- They make plans without giving you therapy.

- They are not happy about the special occasions that they used before to enjoy.

- They don't want to impress you anymore.

- They seem aloof from you.

- They may be having an affair.

There are two ways of being appreciative, one depending on timing, the other depending on the central concern. Somewhat of a concern is time-sensitive gratefulness. Either you have turned out to be increasingly dissatisfied with the actions of your companion over time, or you are getting even more forgiving. Your point of view can rely exactly on how it swings out.

Acceptance comes from the belief that for a time, circumstances are not prone to change, and so you become even more accepting. You would find that it is better to accept what they do as you become more accepting. If you change your point of view, you may find that there may be some merit for even (what used to be) their most irritating habits. What's more, this encourages you to reflect on what can make your relationship happy.

There are so many easy and simple ways to show your partner appreciation:

• Smile at them.

Nothing is better and more productive than looking at someone in love. As I said before, about half the game is verbal contact, but a quick thank you is not always enough. Take the time to look at your companion from your heart and wink at them. The one smile is going to remind them that you are grateful for what they do and the fact that they are in your lives. Without trying to say it aloud, a smile will express a great deal. It would barely take you a couple seconds to smile a few times a day at your girlfriend.

• Start paying attention.

Do not listen with half an ear to what your companion says.

See them in the eye and when they're talking to you, turn towards them. Show them that what they are saying concerns you. Tell them if they had their day. If they said, they were craving food, then the next day, recall offering it to them. Surprise them by demonstrating that the small things are all you pay attention to. Show them that you care and that you think about them the way they think about you at all times. They would enjoy it.

• Show them that you are reliable.

It is important in a relationship that your partner can count on you. Both persons need to be responsible for their acts and for each other to be healthy. They should be confident of the fact that their companion will hold their word and respect their promises. Don't betray the trust of your partner and make sure they know they can rely on you at all times. When you're expected to reach them, don't be late. Don't forget that they wanted you to do something. The way they are to you, be reliable. You can send them some as well if you want them to help you.

• Physical gestures of affection.

Physical fondness is strong. It can make too much of a difference to grab their hands, touch them, or just a quick peck on the lips. Don't hang on and be open of your love; your partner deserves it. In your friendship, it strengthens the feeling of love and affection. To show them love, squeeze their palms. Whenever you may, give them a long embrace.

• Be thankful.

One of the first few lessons we all learn as kids undoubtedly has to say "Thank you." This is that anytime they do something for you, everyone understands the value of showing love to others. There is very little effort needed to say "Thank you," but during the day, you will get several chances to say it. Do not stop thanking your companion simply because every day they do the same for you. Instead, every day, start thanking them to prove that you really value their effort. When they hand you a cup of coffee, say Thank you" and say Thank you" even when they ask you about your day. Other than your wife, how many individuals think about how your day went?

• Be helpful.

For anything that they do, you have to thank them and respect them. It is not enough, though to be happy all the time; you still have to make an effort to do something for them. Do a chore for them if you have time. Go to make dinner for the shopping run. Help them get their job done. Do stuff to assist them to prove that you know they're working hard.

• Make small sacrifices.

If your partner knows that, you detest peas with a fierceness capable of fueling a fly plane enough but in any case, you make them that is the kind of little concession that means you are concerned about their desires and needs. The purpose of such small sacrifices is to explain to your partner that you respect them enough to sometimes place their desires and wishes above your own. This is an intense example of unselfishness in an increasingly self-centered culture that indicates gratefulness, benevolence, and compassion.

CHAPTER FIVE

25 Tips to Build Deeper Connections for Couples

Irritations may become misunderstandings, feelings of pain, resentments, and arguments full-blown. We sometimes let frustration or passive-aggressive actions to violate our once-intimate connection. We encourage ourselves, along with our relationships, to return to laziness or inattention. Where we are laser-focused on our wife and the way to make her or him happy, we are now focused on ourselves and how our wounds might be shielded from our belongings, and even our wives if things turn bad.

If we stay trapped inside this post-infatuation point, our relation could languish in a state of discontent for decades, until it eventually unravels, culminating in two individuals living separate lives. When we came together, it sure is not the kind of relation we dreamed for ourselves. You might be asking yourself: How do I get disconnected? Why can we turn off an extra one? Why does the person I thought was suspended from the moon press every imaginable button on my psychological switchboard today? Couples that have been stuck in a spiral of bruised feelings, remorse, frustration, and reactivity, or even anxiety and apathy, generally have a way ahead of them. They should be allowed to get back into the caring, funny, hot, intimate relationship they had. Let's dive into the content now,

- TIP #1 PRIORITIZE YOU RELATIONSHIP WITH MEETINGS

Any of us would say we're putting our friendship together but are we doing this? Will our partnership and our wife or girlfriend be re-evaluated regularly beforehand for jobs, mobile devices, private pursuits, and other men and women? Are we prepared to expend our resources, time, and psychological comfort to make sure that the closeness, trust, respect and affection we all share with our partner is not undermined? Prioritizing the relationship requires attention and energy. A multifaceted procedure includes all (or many of the other clinics that we outline in this article.

However, if you do not take regular steps to prove that you're committed, your own words don't mean anything you might argue that you prioritize your link. However, we have found a habit that is key to clearing your connection and ensuring that on the front burner you retain the well-being of your connection. In order to estimate how things happen between you—what goes well what can improve, and precisely what you want to work to repair any rifts or broken feelings—that habit is to hold daily meetings with your partner. It is not a gathering to review your kids, your to-do lists, or even your upcoming vacation.

It is a meeting primarily to reflect on your relationship and find ways to make it become healthier and more efficient, and it should be the exact first habit you have mutually developed. When you're going through a tough war or war, you need to satisfy yourself before you feel like things are back on track, and you've reached a resolution. Look at completing weekly or twice yearly, otherwise. Set aside an hour for your conference, even though you don't need the entire hour to wrap up.

The method of building this habit

- Go over per day and a time of day, which works nicely for both of you.

- Establish a reminder program or activate it for the meeting.

- Start small and make it simple.

- Read notes in a diary during the meeting.

- Put the tone for your meeting.

• TIP #2 EMOTIONAL INTELLIGENCE

Psychologist Daniel Goleman points out that EQ can be more important than IQ because standard intelligence ratings are somewhat limited and do not represent the full spectrum of human cognition. Emotional Intelligence: Why It May Matter More Than IQ Our ability to communicate well with numerous people, especially our relational partners, has more to do with our long-term success and satisfaction than our understanding and analytical abilities. The meaning of EQ was popularized by Goleman's novel; however, both scientists and psychologists, Peter Salovey and John Mayer, who invented the modern perspective of what intellect encompasses, originally developed the term "emotional intelligence". In addition to the ability to perceive, interpret and respond to other people's thoughts, emotional intelligence includes the ability to regulate and communicate our emotions. Salovey and Mayer invented a version of four variables, which they consider to involve emotional intelligence.

I. Perceiving Illness: You have to understand them properly to understand feelings. This understanding can include markers of nonverbal comprehension, such as body language and facial expressions.

II. Reasoning of Illness: This measure involves using your thoughts to start reasoning, thinking, and appraisal. Emotions allow us to reevaluate what we listen to and react to and how we respond to those things emotionally.

III. Recognizing illness: There may be many things that may signify the emotions we all recognize from others. If anyone displays frustration, then we have to interpret both the explanation for the enthusiasm and what it could mean. It requires a more subtle skill without leaping into conclusions to recognise multiple possible motivations.

IV. Managing Illness: An important aspect of EQ, particularly with regard to your love affair, is your ability to manage emotions effectively. A part of psychological control is to control the emotions and to respond properly to the feelings of others.

The way to develop this habit

- Begin by clearly agreeing on the EQ custom on which you want to work.

- Write down the low EQ habits of the experience.

• TIP #3 CREATE SYMBIOTIC RELATIONSHIPS VISIONS

Creating a view of a partnership forces you to be conscious and it allows you to identify your priorities and aspirations and stimulates meaning and direction in your relationship. It makes it easier for you to be deliberate and proactive about each aspect of your life together. By first developing and sharing individual connection visions together, you will create a collective vision that prioritizes common expectations and dreams as well as leaves room for the demands of each partner.

The method of building this habit

- When you write your vision, keep these concepts in mind.

- Possession of a strong knowledge of the beliefs.

- For several regions of your relationship, design your vision.

• TIP #4 SHOWING YOUR PARTNER RESPECT AND KINDNESS

Not only is practicing compassion and admiration a wonderful thing to do. In the degree of your relation, it makes a huge difference. It establishes trust and fosters good contact. It helps you to cope more easily with disputes and challenges.

The method of building this habit

- Choose the habit.

- Decide if this unique habit will be executed.

• TIP #5 PRACTICE ACCEPTANCE OF YOUR PARTNER

Look back to all those magical moments when you fell in love with your partner, and you thought he or she was practically ideal in any way. This person was the whole package—exactly what you were looking for. You did not find any flaws, or you were quick to miss or reduce them if you did. However as time progresses, you're shocked to figure out that your partner was mistaken. When did he ever change? Did you guess?

The method of building this habit

- List your spouse's positive qualities.

- Review your listing with your spouse.

• TIP #6 CHERISH YOUR PARTNER

You will need to be able to boost their growth and advancement to better cherish your spouse—to have the social, legal and moral help they need to continue to improve and succeed as an individual throughout the marriage or dating process.

The method of building this habit

- Use a morning reminder

- Make regular small (and intermittent significant) sacrifices to your spouse.

• TIP #7 TOUCH OFTEN

Studies have found that physical attraction interferes with general enjoyment of the bond. In particular, a study published in the Journal of Family Counseling notes that as they display more bodily affection for each other, couples engaging in an intimate relationship feel satisfied with their connection. The more intimacy the respondents revealed, the higher the connection.

The method of building this habit

- Write down your affection requirements.

- Share your listing with your spouse.

• TIP #8 CONNECT AND ENGAGE DAILY

The foundation of a relationship that is cognizant is to be constantly involved and linked like a few. It is a practice that requires daily attention, as it is easy to become obsessed with the daily burden of life, developing a slippery slope into apathy and estrangement.

The method of building this habit

- How disconnected have you been?

- Check the responses together.

- Tell yourself, and everyone else, why you think this is happening.

• TIP #9 MAKE SHARED RITUALS

For your bond, this pays tremendous dividends. By extending trust, affection, romance, commitment, and balance, they foster the pleasure and durability of their relationship. You and your partner undoubtedly have some traditions that involve you. Maybe you read out loud to each other in bed before going to sleep, or you have a tradition of cooking and planning a romantic meal witness

The method of building this habit

- Review events or actions that you'd love to ritualize.

• TIP #10 VULNERABILITY

It includes putting your guard down and welcoming your partner into your inner world through regular dialogue in addition to reciprocal concern for an individual's sense of psychological protection and confidence. There are only two reasons why vulnerability is important for closeness in your relationship, along with the opportunity to connect openly:

- Weakness shows the entire person you're.

- Vulnerability promotes confidence.

- Vulnerable cures wounds.

• TIP #11 BECOME AN EXPERT ON YOUR PARTNER

Because a few are aware of exactly what each partner thinks and believes, when challenges arise, they are not as inclined to be knocked for a loop. For starters, it causes a huge change in their own life when a couple gets their first child, adding new criteria without sleep. In this phase of upheaval as a kid reaches their lifespan, partners who understand each other well and convey about their thoughts, desires, and emotions are not as likely to experience connection unhappiness.

The method of building this habit

- Discover the amount of time you know your partner today.

- Think of what you want to talk about and figure out.

• TIP #12 LOVE LANGUAGES

The very best way to being obvious is to remind the partner exactly what he or she desires and needs to feel valued and loved. Then you tear down a variety of barriers that threaten the closeness that you want to explore by questioning and providing terms and actions to back up the love languages of your partner. Languages of love consist of

254

- Words of confirmation

- Quality time

- Present committing

- Acts of support

- Physical touch

The method of building this habit

- Discuss the way you desire your love languages extracted.

- Select one love speech behavior for your spouse.

• TIP #13 HEAL HURTS QUICKLY QUICKLY

The very best thing you can do to help the long-run wellbeing of your connection will be to resolve some first disagreements, along with the resulting relational fallout, as swiftly as possible. However, when you are both angry, wounded, and confused by a disagreement, it is hopeless to reconnect and resolve in an instant. To relax and launch a quantified respectful settlement to spot some hurt feelings takes time and contemplation. It does not take days, however to

The method of building this habit

- Develop a time – out signal

- Separate and breathe.

- Reflect on your circumstance and your spouse's position.

TIP #14 PRODUCTIVE CONFLICT

We will need to get better at stirring a winning war in order to improve contact as spouses. What precisely does that imply? It involves learning how disputes can be processed and settled in a way that provides easy choices while preserving the connection. A fruitful war does not mean combat is "nicer." Instead, it means acquiring an intentional and healthier technique to work around discrepancies. In addition, that is when the conversation becomes more relevant.

The method of building this habit

- Select the best time for a discussion.

- Begin with constructive language.

- Produce mutual floor rules.

- Listen and confirm first.

- Brainstorm many options.

- Seek out support from other people.

- Reframe criticism as criticism.

- Learn and exercise mend motions.

• TIP #15 CREATE ACTIVE LISTENING

On your link, active listening has tremendous psychological benefit. It gives your partner a comfortable place to communicate their opinions and emotions. When your spouse hears himself speaking, he raises more consciousness about his feelings or the situation at hand and becomes much better prepared to discover a settlement for you on her or his own or to work on one.

If you wish your partner to be an active protagonist, you must be able to do the following:

Enable your partner to dominate the conversation and select the issue to discuss.

Keep attentive to what he or she is doing.

Prevent withdrawing, even once you have to add something critical.

Ask open-ended questions that foster more spousal results (whether or not she desires that).

Prevent early decision-making or the availability of alternatives.

A partner represents what you learned after he or she spoke.

The method of building this habit

- Determine, trigger, and find a time every day.

- Find a subject for every session in the clinic.

- As the host, discuss with your partner the subject or concern.

• TIP #16 EXERCISE EMPATHY

Empathy is a clinic that will strengthen your connection and extend the world knowledge around you. You are linked to a greater, more mindful amount of participation and consciousness by getting out the cocoon of your life, issues, and emotions. If compassion does not come to you easily, or if you have shut yourself off from compassion when you fear it would be too humiliating.

The way of building this habit

- Identify how the partner thinks by paying extra attention.

- Mentally, put yourself in the shoes of your partner.

- Verbalize and visualize how it would feel.

• TIP #17 USE I FEEL INSTEAD OF YOU

One path to cultivating a more aware friendship is by actually modifying a few basic terms about working together and being more deliberate about sharing your insecurities and bruised feelings without realizing criticism or defensiveness. Instead of accusing your partner, you change the entire nature of the way you feel and what triggered your emotions

The method of building this habit

- Consider prior wounds that are linked.

- Concentration of your thoughts.

- Using a statement of "I believe".

- To express outside wounds, use "It reminds me "

- Ask for the service you need.

• TIP #18 REDUCE THE BUTS

"Reduce the Buts Contemplate how it feels when a person tries to confer with you and includes the phrase "but I'm sorry I missed our lunch date; but, I got distracted with the feature "I'm sorry I hurt your feelings; but you shouldn't have asked for my opinion, "The "but" makes it sound like a half-baked admission linked to some insufficient excuse or qualifier.

The method of building this habit

- Begin by finding your "buts."

- Analyze your reply and rephrase it.

- Affirm and usually respond favorably.

• TIP #19 LEARN TO APOLOGIZE IN A CONSCIOUS WAY

Your voice is clear, simple, and unambiguous when you speak to your spouse correctly. There is no pretense of overt contact or a secret message; the purpose is quite clearly to get or provide information and start a conversation with your spouse. This involves the two-way, free-flowing exchanging of ideas, feelings and thoughts in a manner that leads to alternatives. You'd think this would be easy, and for a handful, that is it. Most of us however have trouble expressing accurately in certain areas of our connection; therefore, to be able to convey ourselves, we resort to all sorts of verbal contact. Alternatively, we rub our emotions up until they float in unproductive ways and melt.

The method of building this habit

- Under what ways do you hold back or hold back indirectly?

- To start your practice, choose the least difficult subject.

- Allow the partner to become straightforward without answering, as the listener.

- Request what you need, not anything that you do not want.

- Represent, affirm, and order more as your listener.

- Provide more details or detailed information from the speaker.

- What if I am unable to respect the request?

• TIP #20 MANAGE YOUR ANGER

How much of your discussions with your girlfriend have helped drive you all mad? In our own lives, there are many other people with the power to press buttons and rile us up as our partners do. However, in your relation and your well-being, voicing your frustration from hurtful, self-improvement modes wreak havoc.

The method of building this habit

- Understand how anger seems for you and what causes it.

- Notice passive-aggressive anger.

- Cut back on alcohol.

• TIP #21 LEARN HOW TO APOLOGIZE

Among the most critical things leading to marital fulfillment are apologizing and asking forgiveness. A more powerful friendship will inevitably result from being in a position to proceed through hurtful, unexpected incidents. Partners who know how to give heartfelt apologies to anyone else may expunge the fatal injury and guilt that keeps them from having psychological contact. Apologizing though is a dynamic relationship skill, one that takes careful commitment. It takes doing something that most of us find incredibly difficult— getting past ourselves. Many people either do not apologise, or else they do something with immunity or flippantly.

The method of building this habit

- Focus on your feelings.

- Look closely at your partner's responses.

- Reflect on your actions and explore these further.

- Make sure you act fast.

- Make your apology in person

- Do not dilute it.

- I apologize again if needed.

- Do not stop with a verbal apology.

• TIP #22 YOUR SEX LIFE

Quite a few findings affirm the obvious: the more sexual you and your partner are the greater the pleasure of your relation, regardless of your age. It is enough to have sex once a week to give you a residual spike of pleasure and hold you close as a couple. Along with helping you happier and more romantic when a few sexes have various physical and psychological benefits, you might prefer to stop reading and have sex now. Centered on science, an active sexual life, see the advantages below:

- Increases sum of devotion and psychological familiarity

- Promoting self-esteem and making you feel younger

- Reduces the amount of cortisol pressure in the blood

- Enriches the emotions of grief

- Reinforces a more favorable mindset

- Makes you feel more complete and less irritable

- Relieves stress and decreases depression

- Reduces the possibility of corporal sickness

- Improves resistance and avoids colds and influenza

- Decreases pain by raising endorphins

- Improves general health and burns about 200 calories (a Half an Hour of energetic sexual activity)

- Improves memory

- Generates brain compounds that promote the production of new dendrites

- Improves nitric oxide tone

- Promotes libido for

The method of building this habit

- In your own terms, be confident and gentle.

- Discuss the way a balance can be reached through different sexual criteria.

- Speak about your fantasies or personal sexual preferences as you get more relaxed discussing sex.

- Giving sex a priority.

- Advance your education on sex

- Divide chores for better sex fairly

- Speak about topics that might promote a lack of desire.

• TIP #23 EXERCISE PLAYFULNESS

In part, playfulness is also a desire to be an idiot, which is a mixture of never emphasizing maturity, not being self-important, perhaps not embracing conventions as holy and putting uncertainty and dual boundaries as a source of pleasure and knowledge. The lively mentality, however, positively implies openness to surprise and ability to be a fool, enthusiasm for self-construction or reconstruction, and to retrofit or create the "worlds" that we playfully inhabit. Negatively, playfulness characterized by uncertainty, absence of self-importance, absence of values or some not embracing laws as fearful, no fear of competence, and very little envy

The method of building this habit

- Talk about the problems, which could be supporting a lack of desire.

- Remember your early playful times

- Brainstorm suggestions for playfulness.

• TIP #24 DISCONNECT FROM THE DIGITAL DEVICES

The consequences of our mobile devices may be seen as the dating hurdle of the 21st century, something that our grandparents and parents did not use to contend in their unions. By this broad vortex of digital distraction, they were not enticed away from each other. They definitely had other distractions; nevertheless not one as subtle and counterproductive to true closeness as our electronic devices are very.

The method of building this habit

- Define the limits of the electronic system in your connection.

- Modify your negative habits into better ones.

- Start small.

- Insert new digital constraints and habits in removal.

• TIP #25 LEARN TO LOVE YOURSELF

The spouse's love does not make you whole the foundation for a stable partnership was the linking two entire individuals. If you are not whole, if you do not understand and embrace yourself, then creating this capacity is crucial for your link to succeed. Healthy self-love is a required quality for the two partners as it brings a feeling of flow to your association and love.

Loving yourself requires a mixture of assurance, self-acceptance, and modesty. You recognize your strengths, but without viewing yourself as flawed, you can admit and accept your faults. You accept who you are, where you have come, and just how much more you can improve and improve. You trust yourself a way for other people, such as your family, to get safe boundaries. You forgive yours. You forgive yours

Low self-esteem and too little self-love will jeopardize your relation with several different habits that sabotage intimacy.

That You Should Know:

- Neediness, insecurity, along with people-pleasing

- Continuous acceptance seeking

- Jealousy

- Controlling behaviors

- Codependence

- Reduction of identity

- Blaming others

- Defensiveness and hypersensitivity

- Hypervigilance, intense fear of Earning mistakes

- Passive-aggressiveness

- Perfectionism Bad private boundaries

- Sexual difficulties

- Addictions

- Underachievement

- Workaholic behaviors

- Inauthenticity.

The method of building this habit

- Define with Yourself

- Become knowledgeable of and struggle against your concepts.

- Show compassion for yourself and exercise optimism that is realistic.

- **BETTER FUTURE WITH HEALTHY RELATIONSHIPS**

A healthy partnership is a relationship in which the parties involved feel valued, linked and yet feel independent in their way. Equally, a good partnership has the right to reach out and share your thoughts without someone feeling indebted. When you are in a stable relationship, by the contact and the limits you have set, you will find it.

• Signs of a Healthy Relationship

The right to speak your mind encourages every partnership to succeed because it allows partners to openly and frankly share themselves. No subject should really be addressed in such a situation, and this helps the sides to know as if they are taking their concerns out. In a relationship, freedom of expression also serves to create continuity in a relationship, thereby establishing a more permanent connection.

It does not mean that falling in love means you need to let go of who you are and enjoy every minute with your partner. In order to have time to explore your passions, you need to have your room and yet keep the partnership or friendship as new and enjoyable as possible. In addition, as you grow together as a couple, getting your room lets you grow yourself.

Disagreements are inevitable in any relationship, be it at

college, with your siblings or a couple. Despite how much you would like to persuade us that you are fine, differences are an ordinary phenomenon. If you say that you are in a relationship that has no struggles, so both of you are still standing back and not in your true selves. Even disputes are constructive and generally healthy in a good relationship. That means that instead of attempting to outdo your spouse, you will seek to grasp your spouse by all means, and if you are incorrect, you will be able to apologise.

A stable relationship is based fully on reality. You can't say that you do not like anyone now but say that you love him or her later. Just when you are at the current moment, you need to like yourself and your girlfriend. It is not advised to like anyone in the expectation that they are going to improve. If he improves or not the liberty that comes as part of a stable friendship should hold you close.

Every relationship has a head, which we always claim is the person, but try to make your decisions jointly in your relationship. Often make a commitment to lend an ear to the thoughts of your partner and if possible, even give it a shot so that nothing is a surprise by the time you make a decision.

A stable friendship can be a guaranteed source of pleasure and laughter. Any single hour of the day, you may not be content together when separate things happen, but it ensures that your life together is always loved. Your wife will push up the wall occasionally and you will stomp on her foot, but it will not take long for you to forgive each other and move on because of the love you mutually share.

It is important that there is a harmony in a stable relationship. You ought to strike a compromise with respect to the tasks that you cover. For a business trip, you might need to take care of a sick family member or fly. If your relationship is balanced, you will not dwell on one side, but strive to find a compromise that can make both of you happy and relaxed.

It makes your relationship cute and admirable when you can handle the person you love with respect and compassion. You may be the sort of person that can express reverence, gratitude, kindness and compassion to others you do not even know, or you are not closer to your partner than you are. Be assured anytime it happens that you are not in a stable relationship.

Trusting each other is crucial because this is a critical base. Broken faith is said to be like broken glass. You can patch the fragments together but the breaks will never go away. You can believe that you and your lover have lost faith, that uncertainty will last forever, and it might be a daydream to trust each other.

To be an anchor in every friendship, forgiveness and letting go remain. It helps to develop a friendship and establish liberation when you can let go of stuff and smile together. The freedom created is not to take each other for granted, but to realize that we are human beings and that we are bound to fall. It helps to build a friendship that is genuine without preteens after we collapse and we have someone to tell us that you will rise again without being judgmental.

Nothing sounds stronger than the fact that you are mindful that your fallback strategy is a friendship. You are supposed to be with someone you know, no matter what, you can still come back to them because you are always going to be taken in. You want to think that no matter how wrong something is the one I can let know is my wife because you are in such a stable relationship.

By referring to your partner and not to other persons, protect your friendship. It may seem to be calming to share your marital troubles with your friends and college at work, but they are not in the place to construct your relationship. Your mates can only use your stories during their breaks to build a happy hour to amuse themselves. Do not use your mates as a crutch to get away from hard talks with your partner.

- **HOW TO BUILD AND MAINTAIN HEALTHY RELATIONSHIPS**

A profound emotion that should not be taken for granted is the bond that you build with another human being. You feel happy, fulfilled and better when you are in a positive and stable relationship. Tips to help create healthier partnerships are here;

1. Accepting differences

It is obvious that no matter with how you associate, odds are a hundred percent that you are going to be different. One of the challenges you face when trying to build new relationships is that in their mindset and in their way of doing things, you will find someone who is like you. Knowing somebody is getting you and they get you, particularly if they can see stuff from your point of view, is soothing. If we were all the same though, life will be very boring, with no distinct excitement in being new. Therefore, it is important for you to learn how to celebrate and embrace individuals for who and what they are.

2. Listen

The patience to listen to others is a quality that individuals should adopt because it helps improve the self-esteem of another person. The first step of a good interaction is being able to listen and understand what your partner is sharing with you. Whether you should listen to your mate actively, so your mate would let you know what they think, sound and what your message means to them similarly.

3. Give people your time

When you owe people time, it is a huge present. The planet has turned out a cruel busy place that having someone to support you with his or her time is a treasure. Time is a sacrifice to recognize with the enhanced technology that appears to be a relentless challenge to building relationships with families, acquaintances, and colleagues. It is important that when you owe anyone time, you are present at that time. Without stressing about the past or worried about tomorrow, you need to understand how to be around others. You are associated with the very touchstone of life as you can devote time, resources and commitment to creating and establishing a friendship.

4. Develop communication skills

Communication is not about talking, but it is the opportunity to communicate, because someone else who is listening can hear you. An observation that many individuals make is that the other party knows what you are doing while communicating. The results of bad contact are sometimes permanent and contribute to games of blame, backstabbing and disputes. It is critical that you learn superior communication skills, which will help you, communicate the correct message as expected.

5. Learn to give and take feedback

Giving input is like serving food called progression. Feedback does not always taste fantastic, but in any relationship, it is critical. It helps to tap into your spouse's emotional capacity as you give constructive feedback, thereby helping to forge positive and mutually beneficial relationships. As a person receiving input, you can get free data that you can choose to take or dispose of. Generally, suggestions will allow you to reach into your blind spot.

• COUPLES THERAPY FOR A HEALTHY RELATIONSHIP

1. Interrupt the cycle of negativity

As a pair, you might get into trouble when you fall a series that is breeding negatives. A good example is when your wife comes home stressed; then she tells her husband something snippy. As a husband, you get into a bad mood and you want to stop talking to your partner. Then your wife will believe as if you are ignoring her, and you will not be able to create a normal go-around. You must break it when you are conscious that you are forming such a loop. Like taking a shower, you will indulge in something different. Instead of engaging your husband in a snippy discussion, diversion or relaxing will help you ease the strain.

2. Explore feelings

You have to cultivate the emotions that accompany the cycle that governs you. When you are a team to figure out what went wrong and when, you will do the set-up together. If you make conclusions about those emotions, then you stop talking about it so the depressive loop is feeding what you are merely doing.

3. Understand your own needs and wants

If you are looking forward to a fruitful relationship with someone, then it is vital that you understand yourself entirely.

As a partner, it is important for all of you to consider your personal desires and wishes when you are at the heart of your independent person. If you want to be handled well you need to identify the expectations and then express them to your husband so he does not wonder. It provides a safe practice that will help you better understand and handle each other in a manner that encourages loyalty and social intimacy through knowing what works for you in your needs.

4. Be supportive

You should be respectful of whatever your partner has defined as a need or desire, to encourage things to go smoothly. You can also have very different interests for needs and preferences, so it is beneficial if you can find a way to improve both parties' fulfillment that helps in happiness.

5. Express feelings

All partners must digest a situation in a manner that would not elicit any intense reactions in order to be able to change the toxic loop that occurs in a relationship. To be fair with your mate, do your hardest. It should be easy to articulate your thoughts as much as possible without making space for conclusions. Make it your determination and mission to really listen to what your friend is trying to say. Emotions remain to be a vital aspect of our personalities and identity. In making choices, emotions may be used as details.

Compromise for happy marriages and engagement

Then engagement and compromise are important points to be discussed with the need to manifest a caring, intimate and long-lasting partnership. You have to ask yourself, is it a pledge to whom and what? You have to consider the principles in a relationship to answer this issue.

Taking the example of do we part until death." Which led many to believe in it as a promise. The dedication that this declaration holds such sacredness that readily comes under the weight of satisfying, sacrificing your personal desires, and voicing personal needs. In western countries, there is a significant rise in the number of divorce cases. An explanation related to cases of divorce is that when dedication is applied to the equation, the issue is. Interestingly, despite all these cases of divorce, there is little regard for those who are sad in their relationships.

It is high time to change the attention from the part of us before death to the alive, vibrant finish. In the present moment, create the share together and stop dwelling on what you do not have. Intimacy provides an active link or love bubble bond or land that helps unite the pair and create an intimate space between mates. Any room for love demands focus, caring, and commitment if it is to thrive at all. Caring for the room of love is an obligation and both sides continue to take care of each other.

To understand and develop enough trust, you need to learn what you feel as a person. It is not difficult to disclose who you are between your shadow and light when you have built enough trust. Commitment is the cornerstone on which all discovery will take place. It provides a stable and grounded nucleus through which the deepest layers of vulnerability, alienation and fear of invasion can be pushed through.

CONCLUSION

Communication can make or ruin a relationship. The more the dialog is open, honest, and linked, the more stable a relationship becomes. You are in control of the way you communicate with your mate. Make a deliberate effort to accomplish the above targets, and you can certainly see and hear some crucial changes in your relationship. Unable to communicate with your partner successfully can lead to tension, frustration and even confidence issues. If you can't speak to your partner honestly and openly about something as necessary as your feelings, how can you talk to them about the important things? I read more and more stories of couples that do not discuss their concerns and still only ignore each other, which makes it more complicated.

Finally, you are properly prepared and able to go out there and solve the challenges that are pulling you and your sweetheart apart. On the road, there were many hard lessons to remember, many harsh facts that you had to confront about the ways in which you fell short. That is all right, though! You have come out stronger and smarter for it and you are going to be a hero to your honey. I am still positive that it was a relief to know that such situations are not just your fault. To step up to be stronger, use these strategies; be kind and patient while demonstrating to your partner where they too require development.

Must be mindful of the phrases and behaviors, recognizing that misunderstandings exist. Do not beat yourself up as they do. Apologize, internalize, and evolve! Both of you are only human; forgive one another. Re-evaluate yourself from time to time to ensure that you fulfill the needs of your significant other. Are they yours to meet? Sit down to discuss what needs to improve, if not. Listen, do not interrupt, and never accuse them of intentionally harming you.

Be there with the person you love most in the world, through the good and the poor. Prove your feelings for them by speaking the language of their love. They will come to believe you over time and depend on you again. Have patience! Nothing indicates overnight outcomes. Relationships are as gardens tended to them, every once and a while picking up the weeds and watching the passion grow into something amazing!

Recall these things in short: listen, read, respect, trust, and let things go. I hope you will take what you have been taught here to heart. You would be an asshole not to! You discover, after all the secrets of experts that you will usually pay thousands for! By the way, you are welcome.

This are some of the most powerful techniques you can

practice in your life and in all ways, make the communication between you and your best half much better. However, all these methods take some time for improvement to be demonstrated. Therefore, you need to be incredibly compassionate and compassionate with your partner and strive to be the one who makes the agreement because in the end, partnerships are just about knowing and caring for each other and when you start following these basic techniques with compassion and compassion towards your partner, I can guarantee you that the time is just around the corner that you two can make it.

CPSIA information can be obtained
at www.ICGtesting.com
Printed in the USA
LVHW081058080722
723058LV00022B/241